KNOW YOUR LOCAL

Buckman Publishing LLC
est. 2018
1448 NE 28th Ave
Portland Oregon 97232
buckmanjournal.com

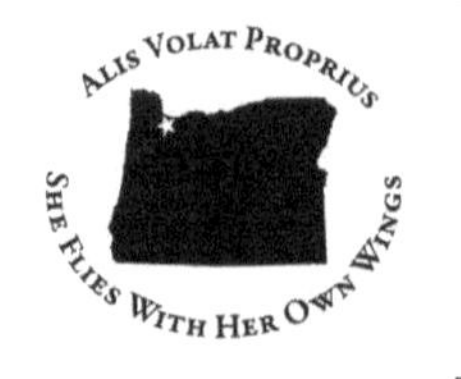


Congratulations! A Buckman production is in your hands! We're an unorthodox operation that continues the daredevil tradition of literature, printing new sparks that ignite imagination. Proudly independent, Buckman's defiant attitude aims to inspire and increase readership in greater society.

ISBN: 9781967058051
Fonts: Garamond Premier Pro, CENTURY GOTHIC PRO, **Cooper Std**



Buckman operates from our home in the upper left of Turtle Island at the confluence of the Whilamut and Wimahl rivers, among the waters and lands of the Cayuse, Clackamas, Multnomah, St'pulmsh (Cowlitz) Umatilla, Walla Walla, and Watlala peoples.

Buck mxn

## Team Buck

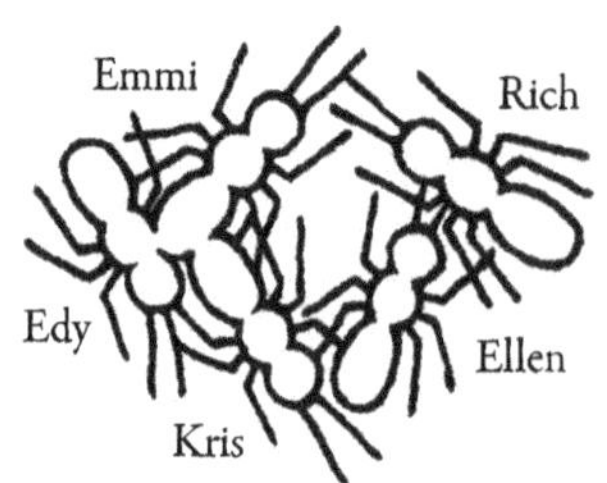


## Cover Info

Photography: Hannah Krafcik
Dancers: Sophia Tweed Ahmad
SOPHIATWEEDAHMAD.COM
IG @_DIRTYTWEEDS
Kenny Frechette
KENNYFRECHETTE.COM
IG @K__E__N__N__Y__
Muffie Delgado Connelly
MUFFIEDELGADOCONNELLY.COM
IG @MUFFIEDELGADOCONNELLY
Writing: excerpt from "Homebodies" by Michael Kurt

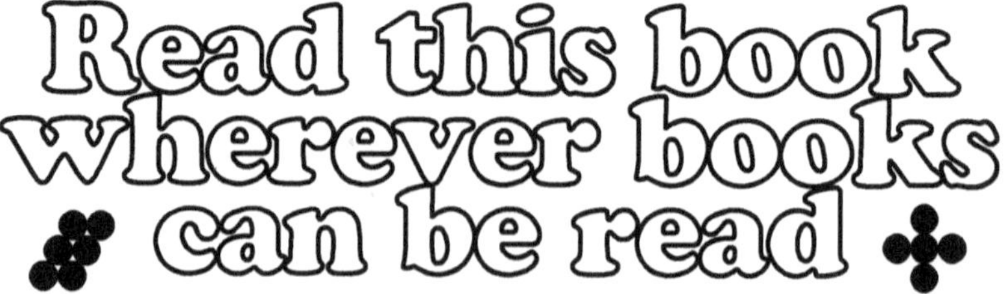

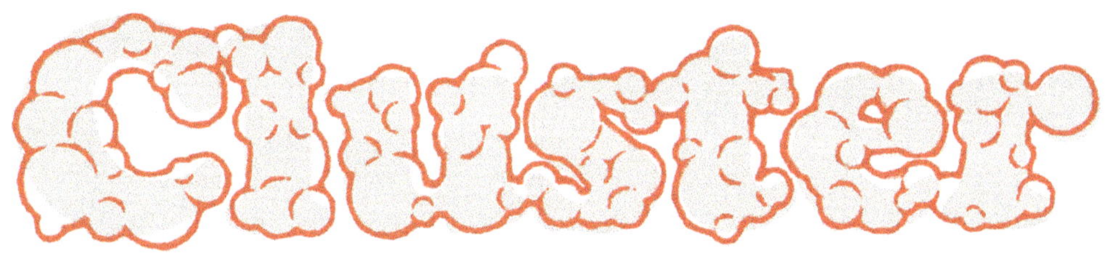


BUCKMAN JOURNAL
ISSUE 015 / WINTER 2026

# CONTENTS


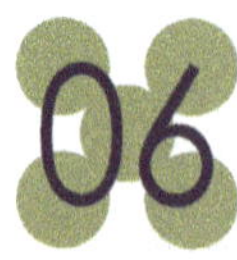

06 LETTER FROM THE EDITOR

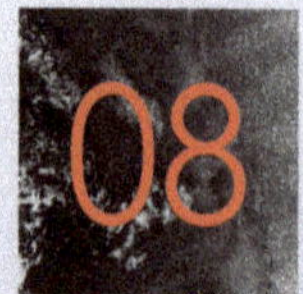

08 THREE GENERATIONS
Words by Joon Ae Haworth-Kaufka / Art by Pearlyn Tan
The matrilineal fabrication, the ghostly inheritance

10 HOMEBODIES
Words by Michael Kurt / Art by Hannah Krafcik
A house of seeds, with walls of people

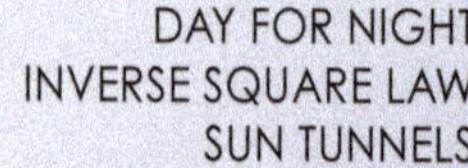

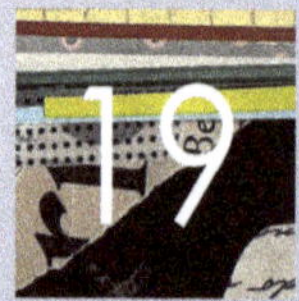

19 DAY FOR NIGHT
INVERSE SQUARE LAW
SUN TUNNELS
Words by Will A.C. Mulligan / Art by Torea Frey
The eye like a literal lens, the figurative come to life

24 BLOOD ORISON
Words by Ruby Wang / Art by Ari Albertson
An anatomical dissection of language

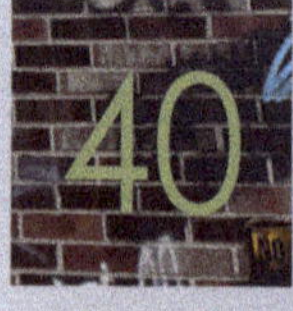

40 MINNEAPOLIS
Words by Rich Perin
The transformation of a townsquare

46 HOW & WHY WE VISIT THE ZOO
Words by Karl Anderson / Art by Kristen Diederich
City animals in their symbolic habitats

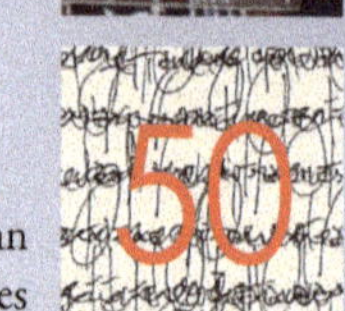

50 Art by Ocean
Asemic writing, meaning in pure shapes

53 BABY'S FIRST JOKE
ASSHOLE
A SINGLE WOMAN GOES TO AN ANNUAL SOLSTICE PARTY FOR THE LAST TIME
Words by Dana Cera / Art by Dan Gluibizzi
Three parts of micro-memoir ft. variations on chicken butt

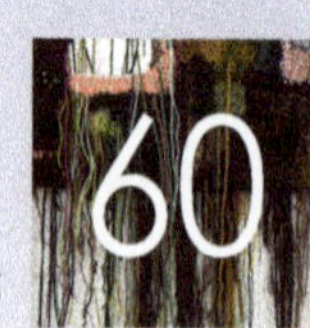

60 APPETITE
Words by Rowan Tate / Art by Jo Hamilton
The fungal gods do their thing

62 THE WHITE PEACOCK
Words by Kirsten Merrell Kippen
A family shapeshifts among seasons, the bird need not be an omen

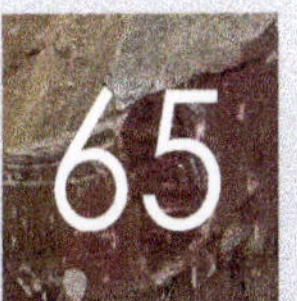

65 SIMONE
Words by Kaya Noteboom / Art by Nicholas Moler-Gallardo
A modern mystic in montage

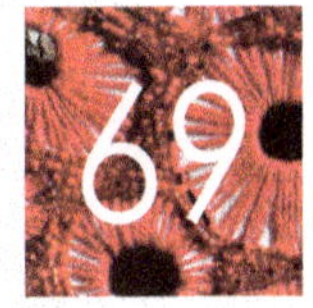

69 Art by Georgia Phipps

70 THE PUZZLE
Words by Milo R. Muise / Art by Jenene Nagy
Longhaul pattern-hunting, as abstract as it gets

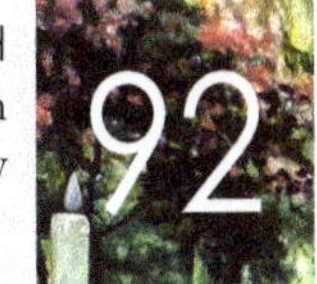

92 TEETH
Words by Thea Prieto / Art by Rachel Warkentin
In the waiting room for grief group, walk into its maw

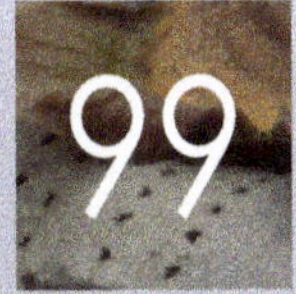

99 ABSENTLY, THE LIGHT
STOMACH LETTER
Words by Emma Riskin / Art by Maxwell Kline
A correspondence between mouth and gut

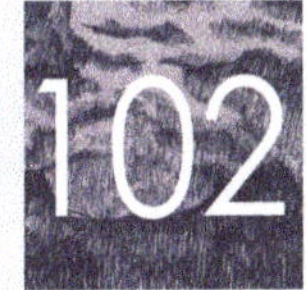

102 OUR SUMMER
Words by Noah Jordan / Art by Taylor Wallau
The downers put a pleasant drag on everything

108 AFTER SUNAN AL-TIRMIDHĪ 1668
NO ANGEL SONG I
Words by Josh Cox
Invocations wait in the wings

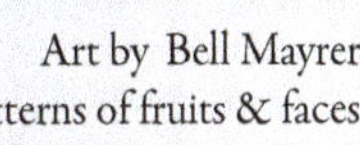
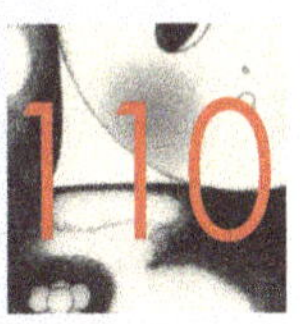

110 Art by Bell Mayrer
Carbon characters, patterns of fruits & faces

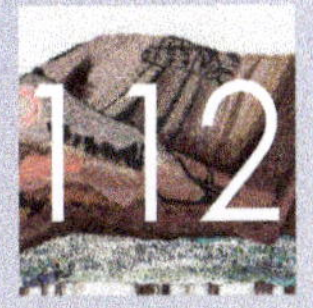

112 BEFORE THE FIELD
Words by Edie Koehlert / Art by Jo Hamilton
Lines of sinuous linguistic proteins

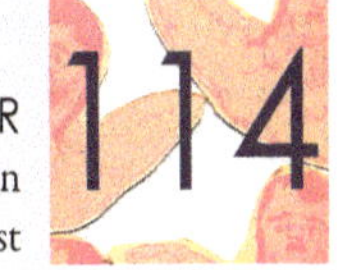

114 BUZZER
Words by Lilly Grey Rudge / Art by Meagan Berlin
The reality TV show palimpsest

125 SO MUCH SO
Words by Harper Quinn / Art by Sarah Meadows
A last conversation, then a ladder

128 CONTRIBUTORS

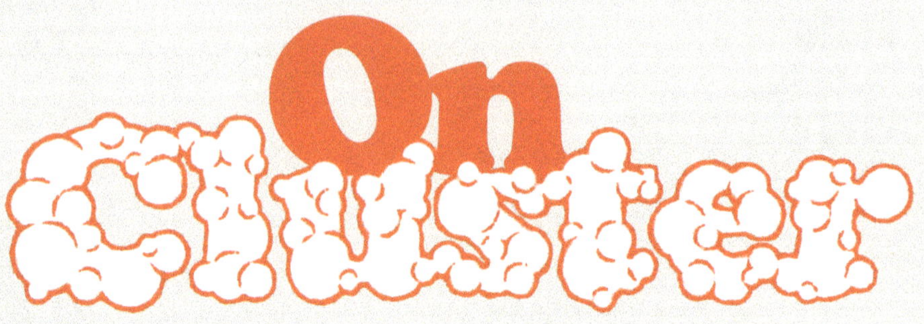


# On Cluster

Picture panicles—a name for the innate inflorescence pattern, how the flowers choose to bloom across branches. See loose pyramids of citrus hanging in their orchards, held in toothsome gravity by a main stem. Or a well-established winter cluster of honey bees huddling hard into their comb. A suite of glossy high-rise buildings glinting sunset off each other. A crew of misfits fit together in the high school cafeteria. Think of gatherings, galaxies, neurons, civilizations. The group chat. The pool balls. Goosebumps. Consonants. Tastebuds. Cluster speaks to association, generation. Putting numbers next to each other to increase possibility. We do the same with sounds and call it language.

These days, it might be lexically best known as part of its vulgar-made-mainstream portmanteau: Clusterfuck. Supposedly first used by poet Ed Sanders in the underground newspaper *East Village Other* in 1965, it describes a situation gone wrong at every angle, which feels hardly hyperbolic in 2025. Sanders was a bridge between hippies and the beat generation, a counterculture stalwart and lifelong taboo-breaker. Sanders published the avant-garde mimeograph journal *Fuck You: A Magazine of the Arts*, so he was well-suited to be the one to make this profane innovation. Clusterfuck resurfaced on Urban Dictionary in 2003 with its now-known definition. In 2005, artist Mike Kelley debuted a multime-

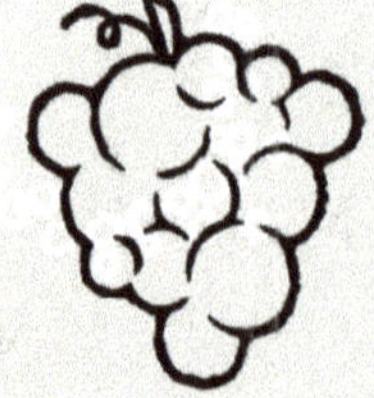

dia funhouse installation, "Day Is Done," which *The Village Voice* deemed an early exemplar of "clusterfuck aesthetics," noting the fondness for overloaded media we have culturally nurtured ever since.

Clusters define us up and down. At the molecular level, a gang of atoms from the same element bond closely together inside their container, the next level where those atomic-made molecules hold together with strong covalent bonds. As it should be, a give and give. Quantum entanglement, can't help it.

Cluster can come in data, compliments, the quintessential grape, long-crushed to supply our most timeless elixir. Plants grow in groups to maximize access in which resources are shared, protection widened. This nearness enhances survival. Same as us, evolving into our hominid collectives—becoming these necessarily social beings. Although the screen has become the fire around which we gather instead of actual flame, the impulse to assemble persists, renews alongside us, interdependent. The point is, we like when it can be more than one, right? And that we need that essential company all the way up the cosmotic scale, apparently. Picture, now, the globular cluster, a spherical star conglomerate.

Out there, when a galaxy is dying, star formation slows for lack of fuel, the whole thing dims, a seeming signal that its life is winding down. Astrophysicists call this quenching. But they've also had to name what can come after that: a cosmic renaissance. They call it galactic rejuvenation. Galaxies can collide and become one, but this is something different. Scientists have seen that even a single interaction, a passing hello between galaxies, so to speak, can reverse the quenching and incite a revival. One dose of closeness can help a whole damn galaxy reawaken. Even in the far-flung three-degree canvas of space, a bit of proximity, of synthesis, might alter everything. That whole galaxy giddies back up, thirsty for hydrogen. It brightens, blinking back at us, and starts making new stars again. ✿

## Fiction by
## Joon Ae Haworth-Kaufka

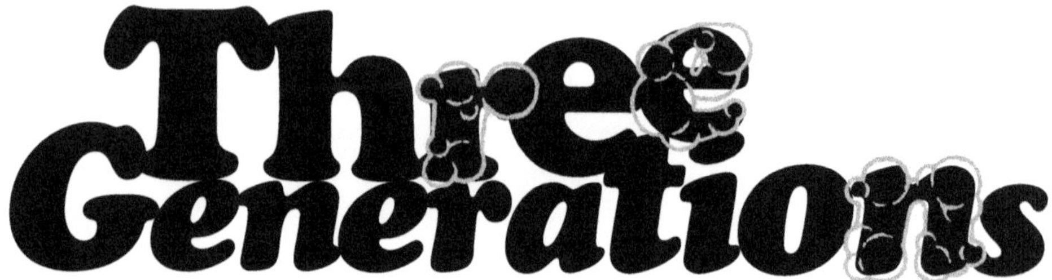

# Three Generations

*Dedicated to Tamara Abu Dayer*

Three generations in one body: you, an egg inside a fetus; the fetus, which is your mother; and your host, your mother's mother, your halmeoni.

It is 1958. The air outside is cold, but you do not know this, only the muffled shudder of your halmeoni's body as she curls next to your harabeoji for heat, both of them bundled in their thin blanket. It is twilight, just before dawn. Your halmeoni is up too early, awakened by the discomfort of her pregnancy with your mother. She listens to the wind whistle through the cracks in the walls and dreads the frigid walk to her sajang's house, a US military man and his family.

You will not know cold for another two decades. In fact, you will be transported to Chicago, USA by plane in the middle of a snowstorm where your new American parents will stand in a crowd of other awaiting parents, holding a small photo of you like a numbered ticket at a deli counter, trying to be patient for their turn.

The war ended five years ago, but its ghosts linger: in the sunken cheeks of women waiting for rations, in the way men still jolt awake at night, in the rubble-lined streets and shantytowns. Hunger gnaws at your halmoni's ribs, and deeper, beneath the hollow ache, your mother exists—a haunting little maw your halmeoni worries about feeding. Your halmoni will eat at sajang's house after the family eats. She is grateful to work for an American military family and to be surrounded by their comfort. Sometimes, there is leftover meat from the American children who refuse to eat what they don't like.

Later today, your halmeoni will scrub floors and do laundry, serve coffee with sugar and real cream to the procession of strangers who will visit the American woman throughout the day, who is said to be a good wife and mother, though she shows your halmeoni little kindness. Then, late

## *Printmaking by Pearlyn Tan*

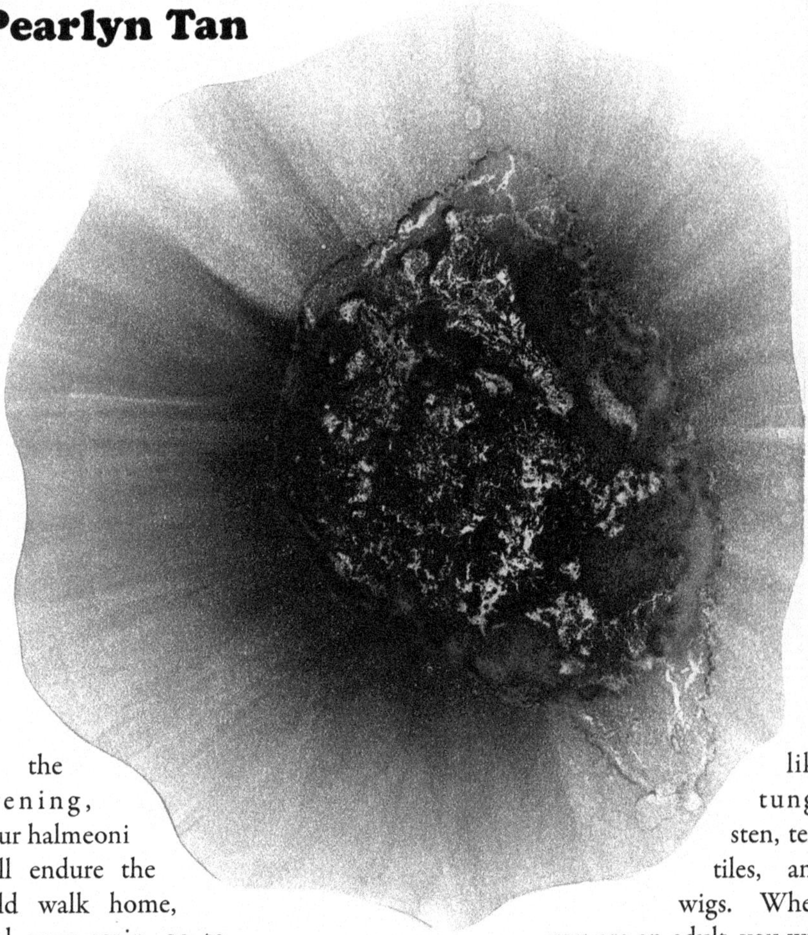

in the evening, your halmeoni will endure the cold walk home, and once again, go to bed hungry. But she is considered one of the lucky ones. They pay her in cash and in rice.

As your halmoni climbs out of bed for the day, she presses a hand to the swell of her belly—to your mother and, in a sense, to you. She does not know you, or that someday, she will lose you. You will never know these people, your family, and their stories of survival. Instead, your body will be trafficked to the US, exported like tungsten, textiles, and wigs. When you are an adult, you will learn that Koreans sacrifice for the nation, and you will wonder, was this a way to fulfill your duty to your people?

Inside the dark warmth of your halmoni's body, a kick lands–sharp, insistent. Her body tightens around her growing baby, where you also float, untouched, unformed. But the world is coming. And when it does, you will inherit its ghosts, its wicked hunger. ✿

*Soft/ Strong*
MONOTYPE (1 OF 1)

# Home

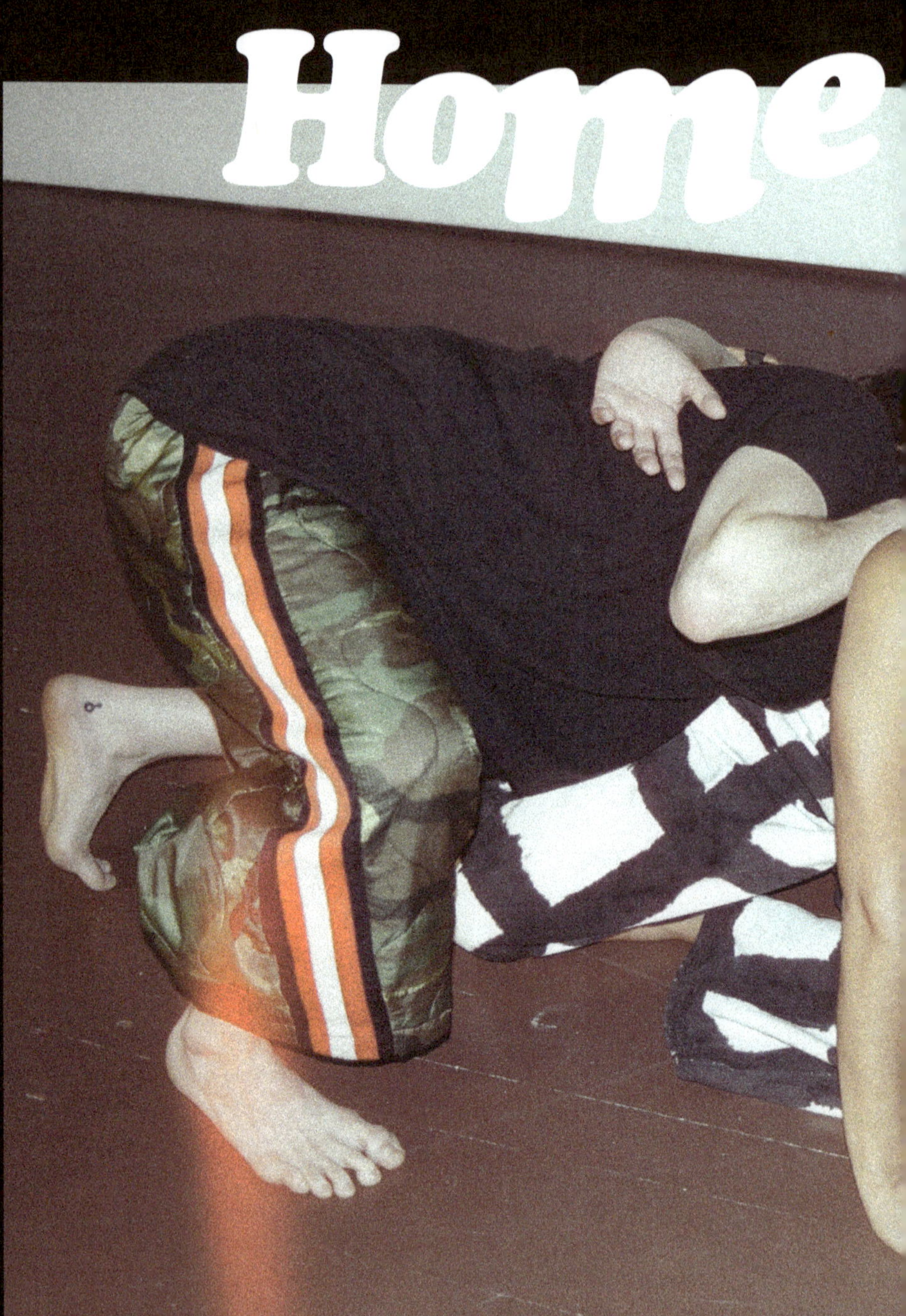

*Fiction by*
**Michael Kurt**

# bodies

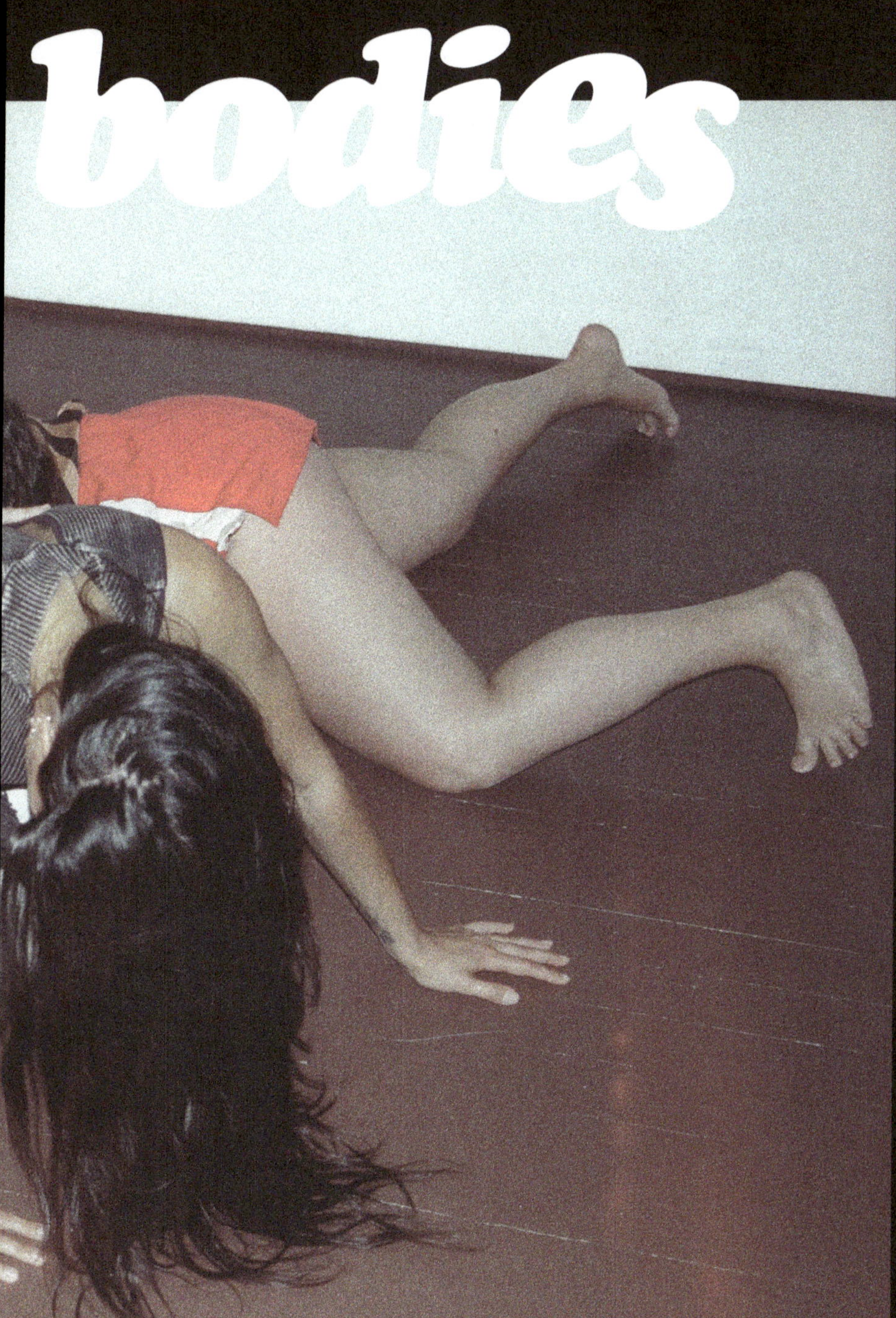

## *Photography by* Hannah Krafcik

KODAK 800 35MM FILM SHOT ON CANDIDO 400

There is something about a bridge at night that makes me want to jump. From deep inside me comes the urge to no longer be part of any structure. It isn't the idea of death, the idea of darkness, or the coming end of light, but something more. Deeper than death, if that's possible.

A wash of red and yellow lights appears on the water from passing traffic, always rippling, always floating away. The impassable nature of night. The steel grating like tiny windows to more steel below, crossing, always holding up. And down, down below, the cement base, a core structure reaching into the earth, through the water, and to the river floor. This will all live beyond me. There's nothing now, but I've seen many things in the water at night.

I walk into a house full of people, almost collapsing. The sound from inside hits me like faraway waves, lapping. The chaos starts small. Someone appears in the kitchen, leaning against the one cupboard I need to get into. Then another at the stove. More people appear in the closet. They push the coats aside, close the door, and after a few minutes of quiet, their voices come through the keyhole; a soft giggling through the crack under the door. A light flashes across the hardwood of the hallway. A phone camera clicks again. It's getting late.

With the kitchen and the hallway closets filled, they begin to appear on the stairs. Two on every step, chattering and laughing, dropping to a whisper after 10 PM as to not wake the neighbors; they

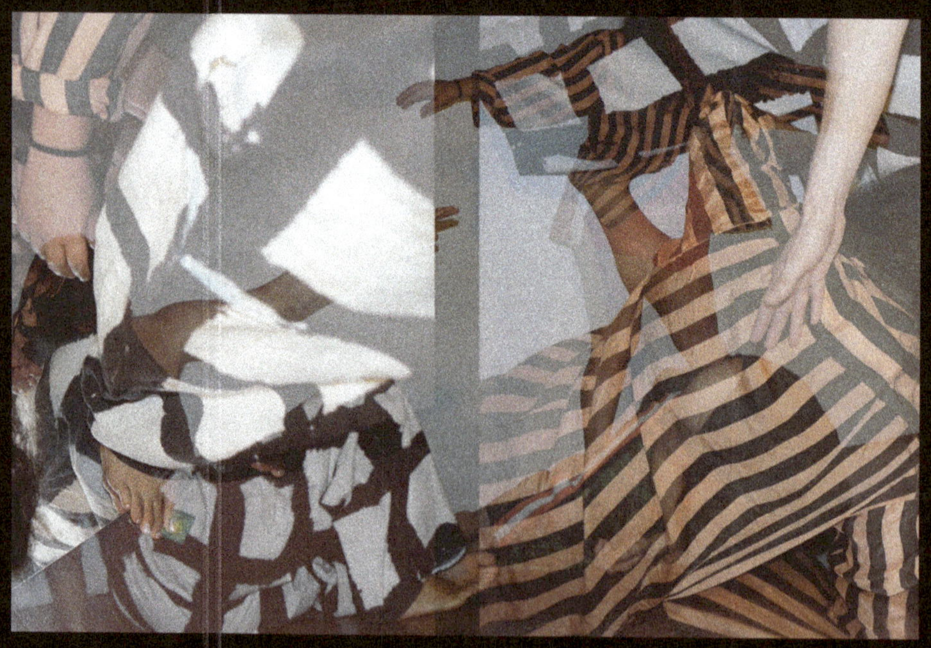

keep me up. In the morning I push through the people. I know their names, but refuse to use them on principle. This will never be their house.

Never do they spill over into the yard, the mailbox, or into the roadway, blocking traffic. I wish they did though, because at least then people would know about the crowd around me refusing to leave. If you passed by the windows, it would only appear as though I had hung dark curtains over every open surface. But those are people. Pressing hard against the glass with their backs turned, crushed up and shaking, like a parade of corduroy and activewear fabrics.

One night the floor gives out and the baseboards crack from the weight of all the conversations. The heat in the room makes the walls sweat through—a marsh basement where there used to be nothing. The people stand in the mud up to their ankles. They say nothing about it, of course, and carry on in the way they always carry on, sinking deeper. I make my way through the mud and the leaves and the flowering weeds along the path I have cut just for myself. They sway like reeds on a riverbank, wind passing through the cracks in the walls of the house, which burst at the creases. They remove the walls to make more room.

The city streets are empty, the cars abandoned, the offices unoccupied. Buses run, but the drivers look nervous, like they'd rather be in the house, like days alone on the cold bus make them dream of a time when they will be crushed together in the mud with the rest of them.

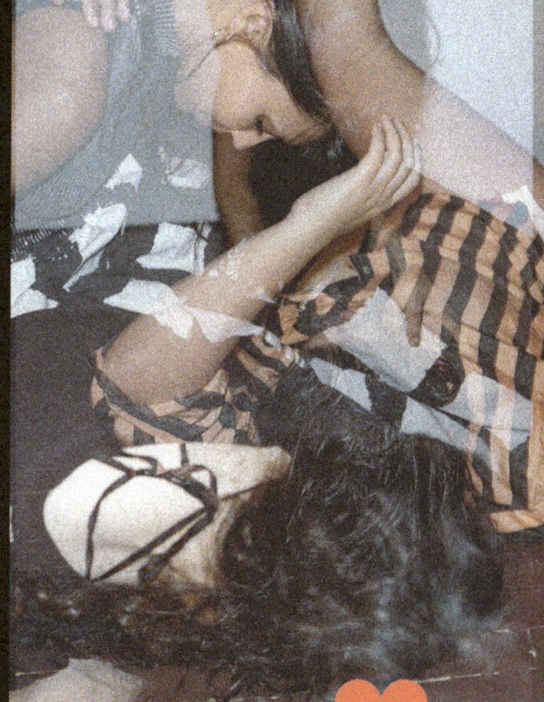

I saw a woman once, walking a dog on the opposite side of the street. She didn't see me. I followed her for a few blocks, knowing, of course, where she would end up. But for a moment—just for a few blocks—I imagined her alone in the city, like me, free to go wherever she liked.

An empty street in an empty town with empty windows. Animals come to rewild what we took from them. Behind old shop windows, grass comes up through the cheap

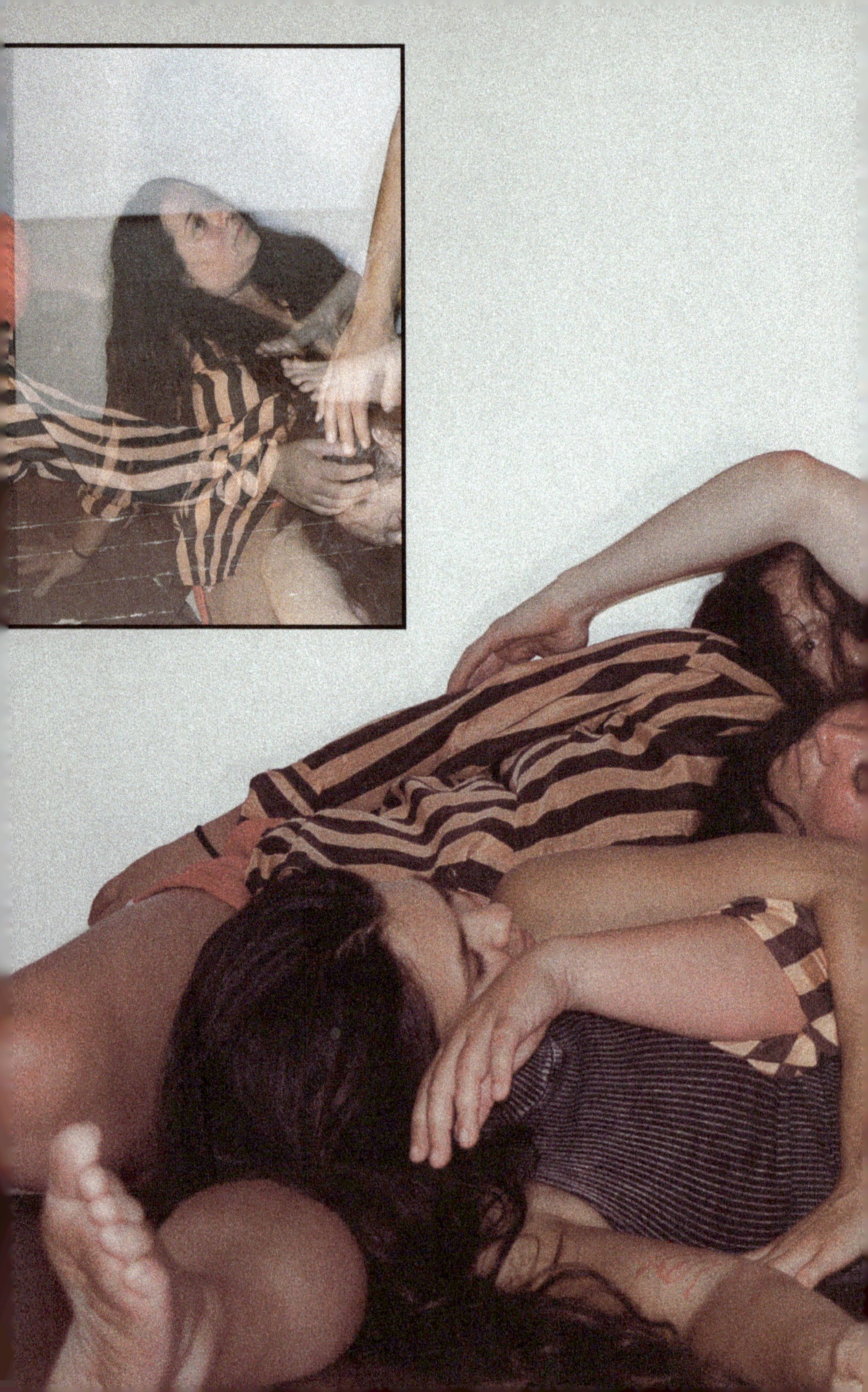

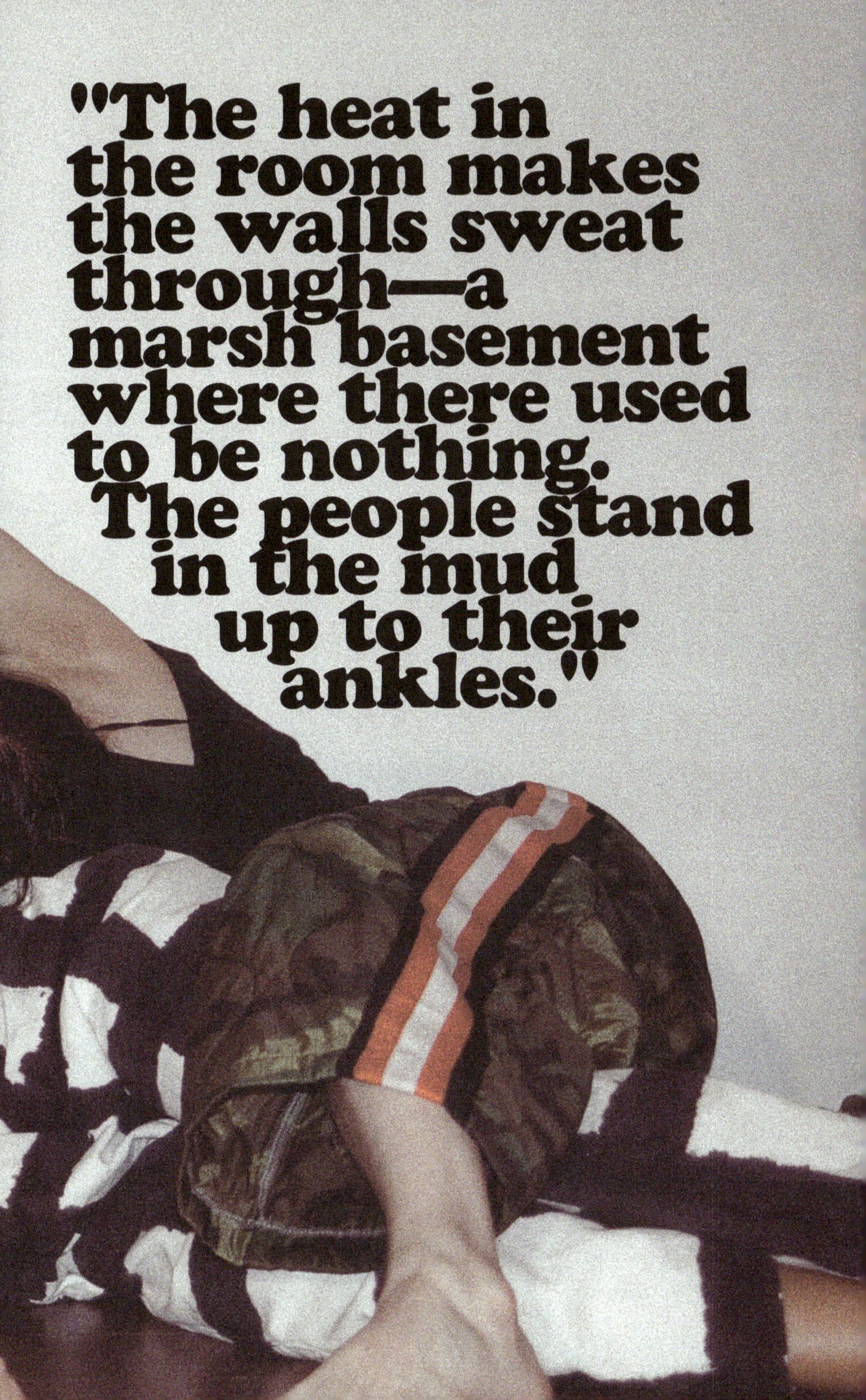
"The heat in
the room makes
the walls sweat
through—a
marsh basement
where there used
to be nothing.
The people stand
in the mud
up to their
ankles."

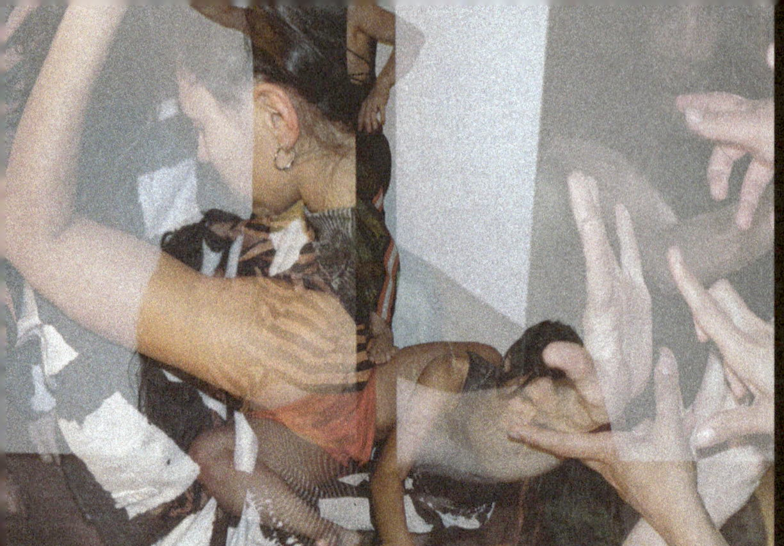
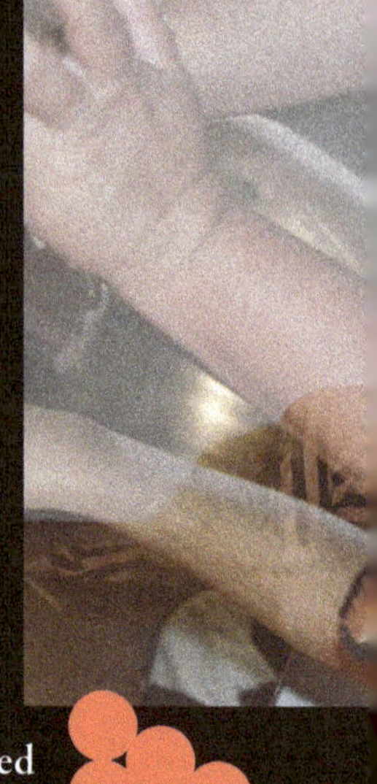

flooring to make tiny black and white subway-tiled mountains. I watch a building collapse from disuse. It simply falls over. No one left to take care of it; no reason to stand any longer. The sound was incredible in the empty streets, a cacophony just for me. The birds come too, made curious by the loudness of collapse. I notice they've gotten bolder.

It feels strange to be out of the house now, like an invasive species trying to grow in a place that has always been naturally balanced. The soil rejects my every step. Trees grow in the house and out of it and fuse with the people, and trap them. With no more space left, they begin to stack into giant columns of arms and thin legs. Human trees. Human leaves fall in autumn now, deceased. But somehow I make it out. By miracle, I'd guess. I want to sleep in the yard where no one else wants to be. But I return to the house, despite there being hundreds of empty houses in town, because I need the warmth of the people to sleep.

I've tried to leave.

But the seeds of the house grow into leaves and bust the seams of antique floorboards and electrical wiring, pipes cleared to make more room for people.

I don't want to be at the top of the column but that's where there is space. So I enter the house through the only door left and wade in. It's tight. It's sweaty and damp with the humidity of a million people too close. Their breath, if they are breathing, hot on every part of me. I remove my clothes because I keep getting caught on something damp. I start to sweat too. The tepid wet of skin against my own, and the stench I know will soon be mine rubs onto me and pushes me through, further into the house. One inch at a time, one tiny step, pushing. I feel their hands and the hair of their arms helping me along. Some of them have fallen almost completely into

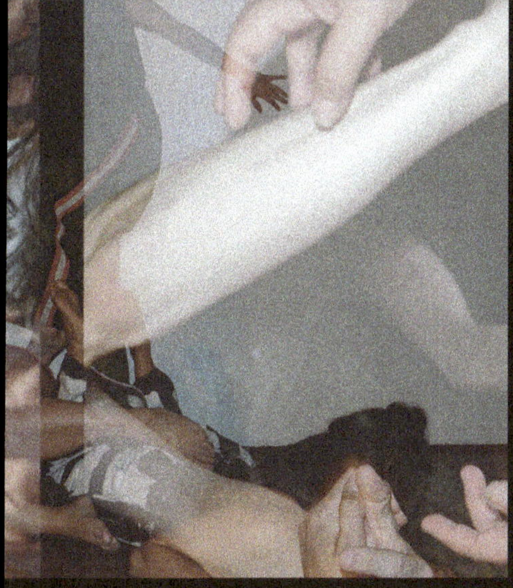

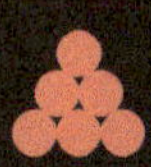

the mud of the house, so much so that I can only see the tops of their heads: long straws like horsetails make their way into armpits and around necks like scarves, and into the mouths of other mouths breathing.

I am pushed toward the kitchen, where it all started. I recognize it, but only a little. Fifty hands meet to form an archway around the open door of the refrigerator. The table, the shelf for the coffee, the stove, the toaster, and the entire counter are gone. But the refrigerator is still here, the only cold in the house, working hard. I get in and close the door. From outside I can hear a pile of bodies fall. Slapping, wet skin. It's scary at first. But as the light dims and the air grows cold around me, I am able—at last—after many days—to close my eyes and go to sleep. Calm, calm, cold, and asleep.

At last, I dream of a world full of people crossing streets. Filing into offices and sitting quietly. Coffee is on in the break room. A heating unit buzzes in the background. The leftovers are thrown out on Fridays, no exceptions. ✿

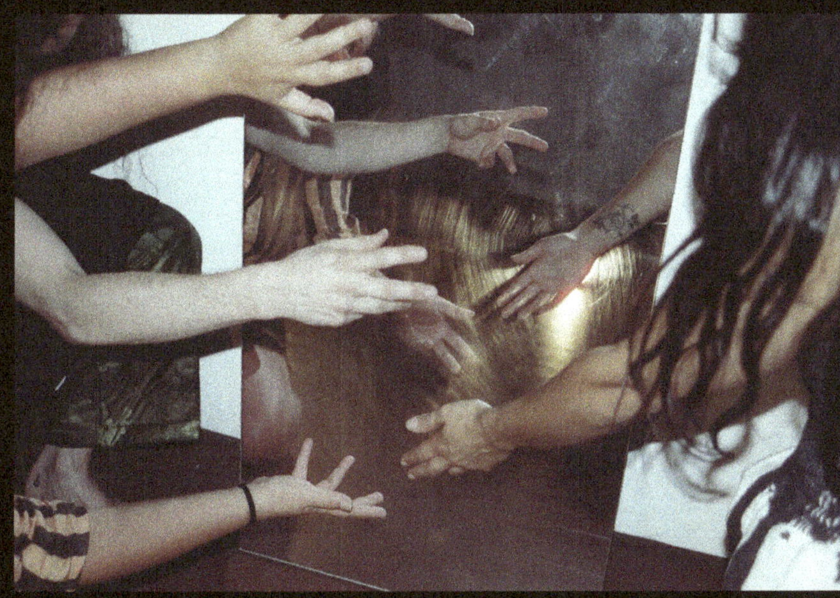

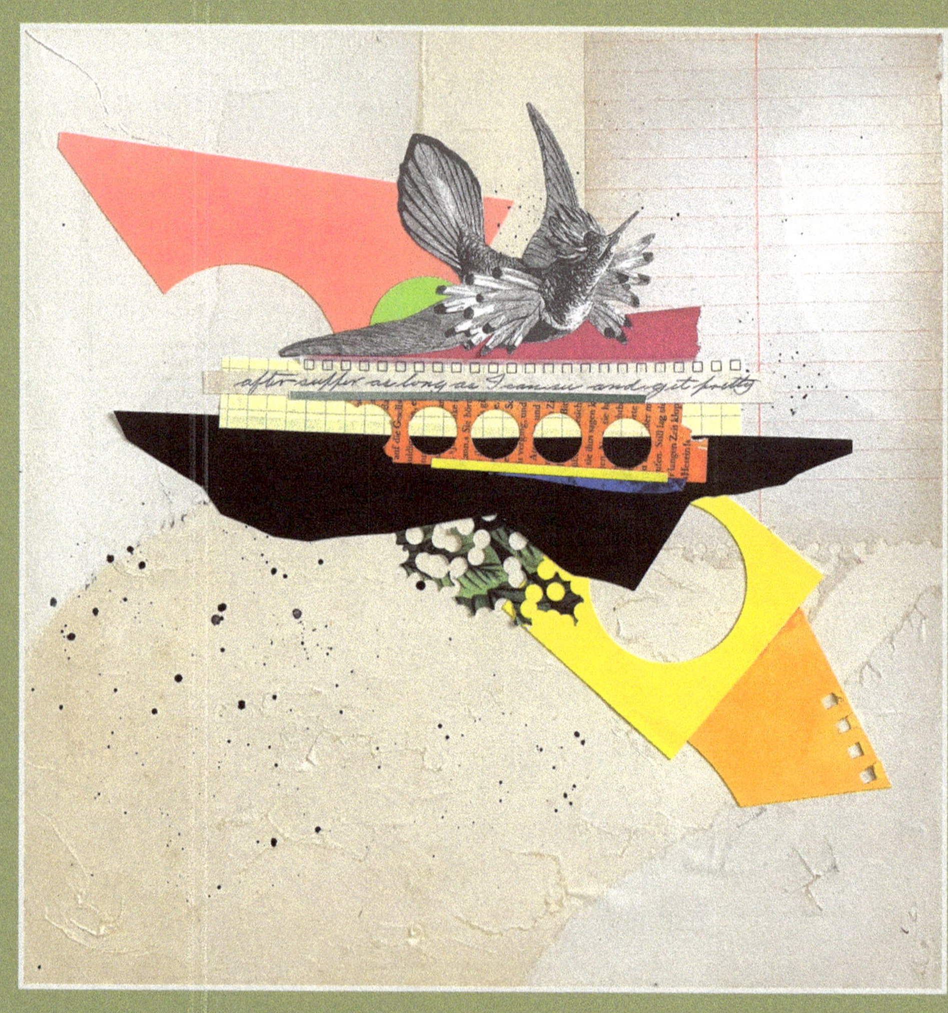

## Mixed Media by Torea Frey



*Behold the Flying Clusterfuck*
INK, VINTAGE AND FOUND PAPERS, PAPER PUNCHES, AND YES! PASTE ON CRADLEBOARD

## *Day for Night*

In any case I don't know how to break the news that In most
cases no news is good news but in this case That's not the
case if I can put it this way we put the Children to sleep like
dogs and the dogs to sleep like Children as was the custom at
the time we tried to Underexpose the sensor so the shadows
well up on The ruby and sapphire display the grit in the
celluloid Graded blue to mimic dilation another clever illusion
Of diminishing vision for finer control of the effect we Can
reset reshoot we can readjust the camera to Create a door
within a door for dogs a frame within
A frame for direction a mirror within a mirror that Gradually
greens until its the best hue for compositing The inherent
power dynamics the camera creates Because blue suggests
night or attempts to render The viewer suggestible to the idea
of shining lights Through soundstage windows to suggest
daytime They told me I wouldn't feel a thing when they
pulled The focus from under our feet what I referred to then
As real bombs with false shrapnel a fine mist of Nostalgia
settled over the mezzanine as required by The form I signed
to gain entry here I smiled because I was on camera I'm sure
this is all coming across Terribly the only way I can think of
to say it is as a Contraction of the soft tissues a shot in the
dark an Impression made in sand where the inauthentic is
Authentically reproduced and put to much better use

**Poetry by**
**Will A.C. Mulligan**

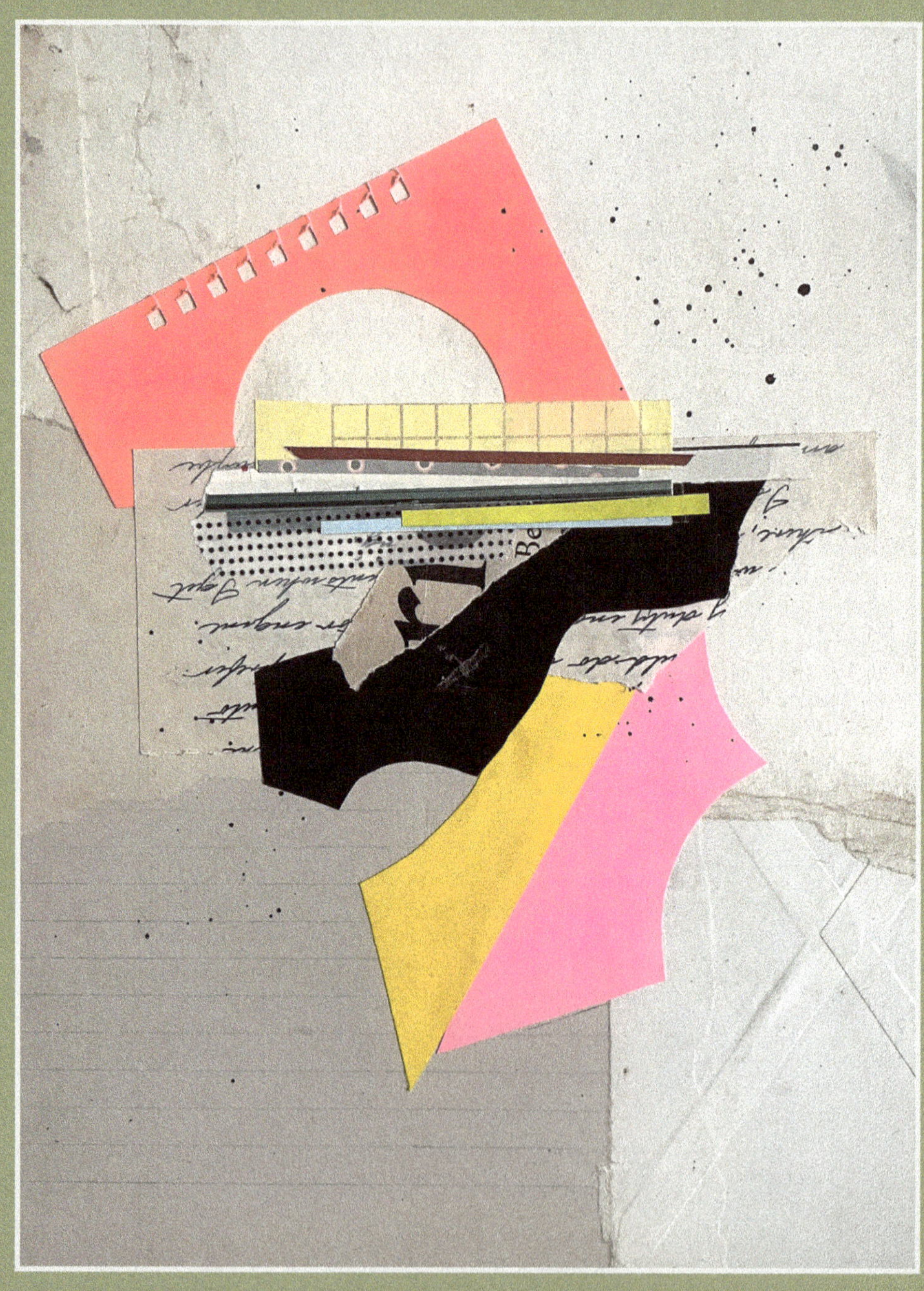



*Be Still the Chaos Engine*
INK, VINTAGE AND FOUND PAPERS, PAPER PUNCHES, AND YES! PASTE ON CRADLEBOARD

## *Inverse Square Law*

Underneath your tongue
A chiral desire for
Desire escapes your doubt emptied spine
To inhabit its own method
Rendering indistinct the prism
Sewn space where confusions resolve a denser vision
Simultaneously delayed as it expands
Knitted into a gentle riot
Braided hands draw the shoulder Blade
that dull knife of desire cutting
                                    Some inside color apart
                    The slow rushing of it
Inconceivable outside the room That
ceilinged garden that collapses
Because every integration is an after
And one was a word for the rigid curves
The tender estuary an intention Stirring
the prairie of your back
A metaphor for metaphor encircled by smirking intervals of skin
Building a field of blood vessels into understanding
An intelligence that pervades the Pause
shaped sounds afloat on the Intangible
edges of the foldable sphere As sinew
and sense oscillate
The collected follicles sigh
Gnawing the gradient wrinkled
Sheets the reactive surfaces Slick
with phosphenes
Where gold flecks green

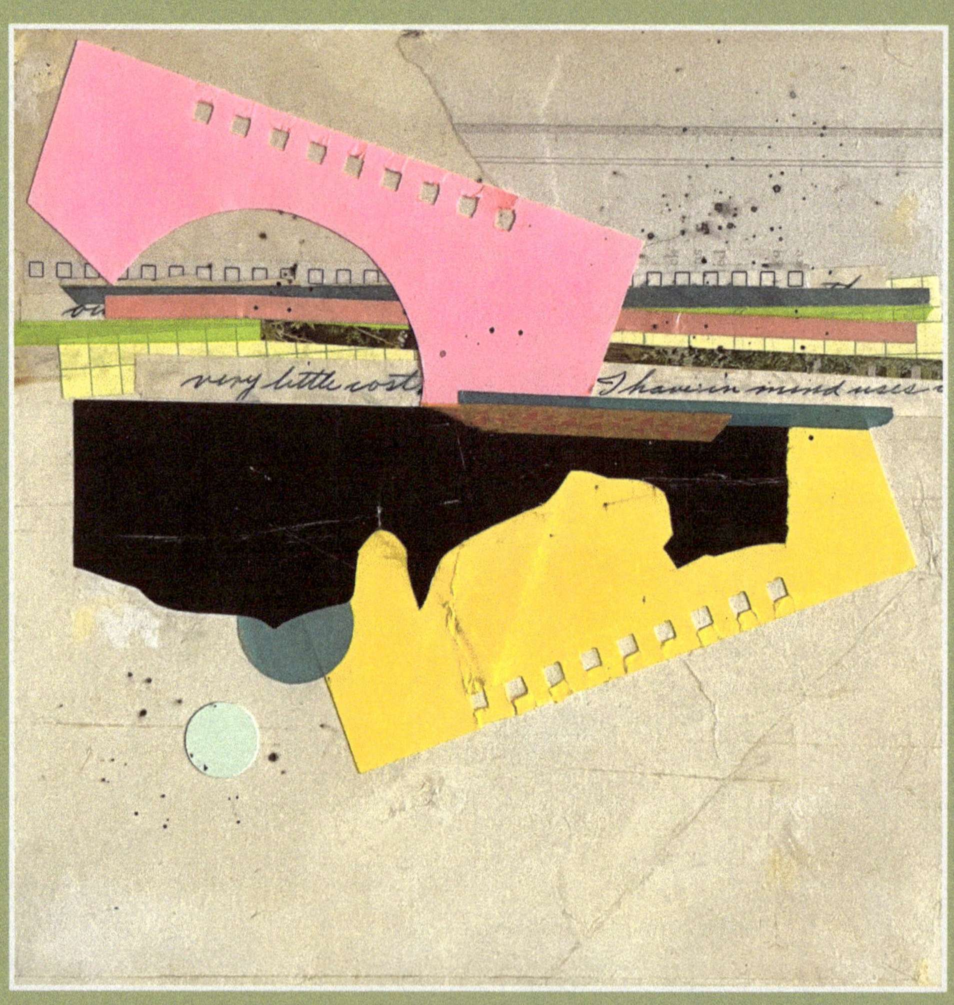


*The Cost of This Chaos*
INK, VINTAGE AND FOUND PAPERS, PAPER PUNCHES, AND YES! PASTE ON CRADLEBOARD

## ***Sun Tunnels***

*After Nancy Holt 1973-1976 (Concrete, Steel, and Earth, Great Basin Desert, UT)*

Back inside after watching sets of headlights precipitate From
the fog. Though I am not in that county, I am count
-ing the stars that are invariably there, reproduced in Miniature
by the light of our nearer star. A scale model of The cosmic
spine with few minor approximations. I count Down from one
trillion until the stellar motion becomes More than neutrinos
passing through complex geometries. You can't make a space
for contemplation in the particle Collider without the empty
space empty space takes up. The Lake of the void spits
overhead. As a child in the suburbs,
I thought English was my first language. Later in the novel
I realized it was time, or rather an entropic gradient coupled With
memory, which makes time visible to me as a past I must Have
moved through to get here. Here I am in the hotel, Accounting for
the area under the curve, hunting for a point To call present, a
point where lines without slope remain Divisible by zero. I'm
looking out the soundhole of the guitar At the snow dusted
mountains occlusion makes. I'm beside
Myself with interference when I look up from the constellations, Unchanged in
the familiar ways. A door opens and closes in
The carpet, a sedimentary sound. What this is, is the internal Math
surfacing with gas bubbles in the blood. It's been a long Time
since time. My shirts cover the floor. The socks are around. My
jeans I don't know. What is now was before in another Shape. If
not, I'd be wearing clothes. I'd have one more organ.

**Fiction by**
**Ruby Wang**

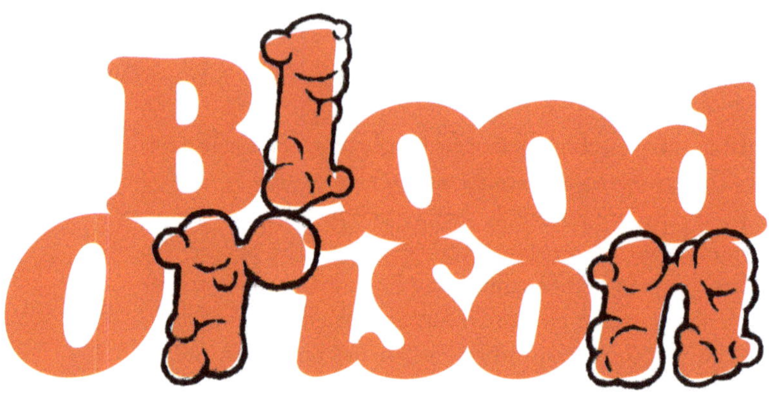


During the day, I am a physician performing surgeries. At nighttime, I isolate myself to string words into sentences. Both roles require destruction to repair what's been broken, but I prefer the forming of language because it's a more demanding, intricate task. "Doctor" was one of the first words I learned. I declared early on: "I will be a doctor!"

Writing emerged much later for me. As a child, I had no concept that "writer" was a thing you could become. The words in books seemed magically formed on the page. Me, compelled by the commanding order of language's flow: sentence followed sentence, meaning begetting meaning.

I was a new student plopped into a foreign classroom. Still, I dutifully observed the budding comprehension of language. Context clues: an unknown word discovered simply by being surrounded by meaning. Familiar language formed the unfamiliar. Yet, I would fail then fail more. Meaning rejected me, refused to communicate itself in my presence. All I understood: words belonged and lived on the page and pages beyond it–those delicate white canopies on which jet-black ink pressed against and danced upon. Teachers informed me how letters in neat rows corresponded to certain sounds and meanings. But regardless of how the letters enraptured me, no sentence made any sense. I resorted to forming a sense of language term by term, the most banal, rudimentary way. And so English assembled itself through letters, then *hellos, thank yous, goodbyes.*

Children, as little humans, are

## *Sculpture by Ari Albertson*

constantly clawing for parts of the world they identify with. I remembered this act of self-expression flooding through the children of my classes. Adamant about their favorite color or protection over a newly acquired playground rock. Squeals to sweets and giggles about nonsense that was entirely coherent to them. Their language formed their personalities on the cusp of emergence. My language lacked any concept of color or joy, no words for self-description. I became defined by my failures in expression. Others used context clues to perceive my inscrutable disposition: slitted black eyes, flat nose, odd clothes. When they needed to address me, teachers elongated the syllables of each word, but their slowness could not coax any meaning out of me.

I dream without a language. Conversations and events pass at night without Mandarin or English. Even though dreams don't mean anything to anyone else, in fact, they're boring, people still speak and write incessantly about their own dreams. I'm guilty of the same. When I wake after a night of dreaming, the first thing I do is record what I saw, inserting words into a picture. I know I corrupt the image a little, altering the dreams from that perfect state of being obscure, hazy images, into a few sentences. Who cares though? Like I said, anyone else finds them boring. They don't mean anything to anyone. Besides me. I write it down because without doing so, it'll disappear from memory and seep into my unthinking rock of a skull.

I used to dream of becoming a

white girl. I wrote down: *that desire to become white comes from a desire to be liked.* Before I fell asleep, I would lie in bed and promise to act like a good girl if God would make me white. Besides the external appearance of my face, I carry internal traces of evidence that I belong to a perpetually foreign being. I am of the genre of persons with insides battered by impossible wants, conjuring folly prayers of a different life when awake, and then only in sporadic, restless sleep do these visions realize themselves. Race, not only distinguished by your own skin but by that impossible want to inhabit another's, so impossible I turned to asking the impossible God about this haunting arresting image of a non-self. Asking scattered like obsession: prayers, dreams, and writings. Practicing this art of asking, I wonder: is the meaning of my dream describable? Have I understood it? God, please tell me. God, you didn't turn me white after all. Still, I trust you, God, no matter how false you might be. So I write nonsense and I'll write it down with a sense of duty.

I grew up in a rural town in North Carolina. We pulled into our new driveway during the middle of autumn, when the leaves were turning gold and red. The air was drier and I thought it might be because the people who lived here were bigger with bigger lungs, everyone inhaling deeper breaths, sucking up all the air. Our neighbors were men with thick muscles and pink skin. They wore less layers in the cold. Other unfathomable parts of our new life: the cheese! My mother could not understand the adoration of cheese and the copious amounts of dairy consumption. My parents' tongues never accepted the pungent flavor of cheese and their stomachs ached whenever they ate it. Always felt too sheepish to ask to subtract the cheese. Always tough, rugged responses to their seemingly ignorant, inane questions in supermarkets and restaurants. How to order? Where to pay? To weather this roughness better than her, my mother forced

> "MY PARENTS THOUGHT KNOWING ENGLISH WOULD PROTECT ME, AND THEY FEARED THEIR HEAVY ACCENTS...

> ...AND MISPLACED PRONUNCIATIONS WOULD RUIN ME LIKE A DISEASE IF THEY TOUCHED ME."

me to eat all the cheeses of America and put me in fewer layers of clothes. When I grew up to like cheese, swiss being my favorite, my parents said they "couldn't understand me."

I devoted most of my youth to language acquisition. In my earlier years, I built a robust vocabulary. My parents thought knowing English would protect me, and they feared their heavy accents and misplaced pronunciations would ruin me like a disease if they touched me. They refused to exchange a word of English with me. After I mastered the *hellos* and *goodbyes*, I learned the vocabulary of foods, animals, and furniture. But a gulf remained between me and my classmates, who spoke of cartoons on television and lyrics sung by pop idols.

Once, my teacher met with my mother during a parent-teacher conference. She echoed my mother's concerns about my struggles to fit in. After the meeting, my parents began to devote a portion of their slim paychecks to cable television. They hoped each hour I watched could transform me into the other children in my classroom. Maybe my prayer about becoming a white girl would soon be answered! My parents were becoming more American too, relying on a purchase to solve their problems. I deformed myself into their perceived American routine, spending solitary evenings staring at the glowing screen, joining the pixelated adventures of Dora in the animated Amazon. "Backpack, backpack!" I yelled back to the glowing screen, grateful the animated images didn't care how different I might be from everyone else.

Besides the television, I acquired language from reading. I graduated from picture books to grade-school chapter books hauled from the local library, then eventually, I caught up to everyone else. In class, we read Shakespeare and John Steinbeck and Toni Morrison. I was reading as much as the other students, then some more. James Baldwin, Charles Dickens, Virginia Woolf. My parents would say, "that's enough, you can stop reading," but it never was enough. I read translated stories from the world, even the Chinese ones about what life looked like for my parents, their parents, and the people before them.

The more I read, the more I learned about the lies we tell. For instance, a misconception about the color of blood being blue beneath the skin, only becoming red when exposed to oxygen. I too believed blood was blue, only later realized the statement as untrue. And yet, the lie seeped into me and still I imagine myself blue beneath my skin. Science and fact and all that adamance about "truth" can't always reconcile the tension between inside and outside.

Lately, I see more and more patients reject the authority of science. People denying treatment, saying no to medication, ignoring statistics. Refusing to concede our authoritative hand to entropic nature. Faced with an expression of misery, I also wish to don the face of God, to fabricate the miracle of good news for my patients.

It takes at least seven years to become a doctor. For me, it took a decade, and in each of those years, you're drilled to follow a strict intellectual regimen. Just knowing as much as you can about a heart takes at least a decade and possibly a lifetime. How exactly will you stop the heart from doing what it wants? I still can't fully answer this.

The heart's anatomy maps itself in my brain as I obey the precise actions required of me. The entire process follows a meticulous procedure based on certainties: the minutes after a heart attack, the orientation of a particular valve, the thickness of your heart's muscle. But still, I'm not a God, and I can't make the heart bend to my will.

I've found that writing is the closest to playing God we can manage. Ironically, my success as a surgeon contradicts my writing. The formation of fiction has no procedure, no anatomical demands. When I write, my motives move against any process. Instead, I'm dedicated to nonsense. Each story contains hundreds of lies.

As I form each sentence, I slice a thin line through, releasing the chamber's contents of syntax molecules expanding and collapsing on itself. Blood spills and the satisfaction of error fills me. Little mistakes splatter on the page. My fingers click on the keyboard like a killer maniac stabbing with their favorite knife.

A good writer makes the character's motivations clear. "Out of character" happens when actions are inconsistent, clashing with whatever motivations were initially outlined. A good writer is also bad at wish-fulfillment. Despite what the character wants, their motives and desires cannot be fulfilled. Not until the very end, at least. Conflict arises when the plot contradicts desires, and actions result in unforeseeable consequences. Will this story have a happy ending or a sad ending?

A good heart makes its intentions clear: to live. An ornate system of arteries and veins fulfills the operations of the heart, its sole motive of attracting blood to continue beating.

Sometimes, the valves and muscles act out and refuse. No language speaks on their behalf, saying why their motivations contradict the rest of the system's. The



*SYNOVIA* (two)
STONEWARE, GLAZE, AND UNDERGLAZE

heart, who wants nothing but to be a good heart, cannot help but ask, *why can't you fulfill my wishes?*

I mirror the decorum of my patients, though most of them agree to skip the formalities. Many times in my examination room, we do not bother with the exchange of *how are yous,* as the moments preceding my impending diagnosis have been marked by uncertainty. Their disregard for politeness means *let's just get it over with.*

For most of my life, human emotion confused me. I continue to struggle with swings from rage to emptiness. Only during moments when my patients burst into tears or their expression suggests fury do I experience a clarity about human feelings. Reactions, like mathematical equations, can be predetermined, solved in absolute rights or wrongs. A few of my words unleash the joy of relief or the hurt of grief. When I reveal bad news, I later blame myself for the inflicted pain, wondering if I could've done a better job. I've grown bitter by words, how the fabrication of a few could ease all the pain.

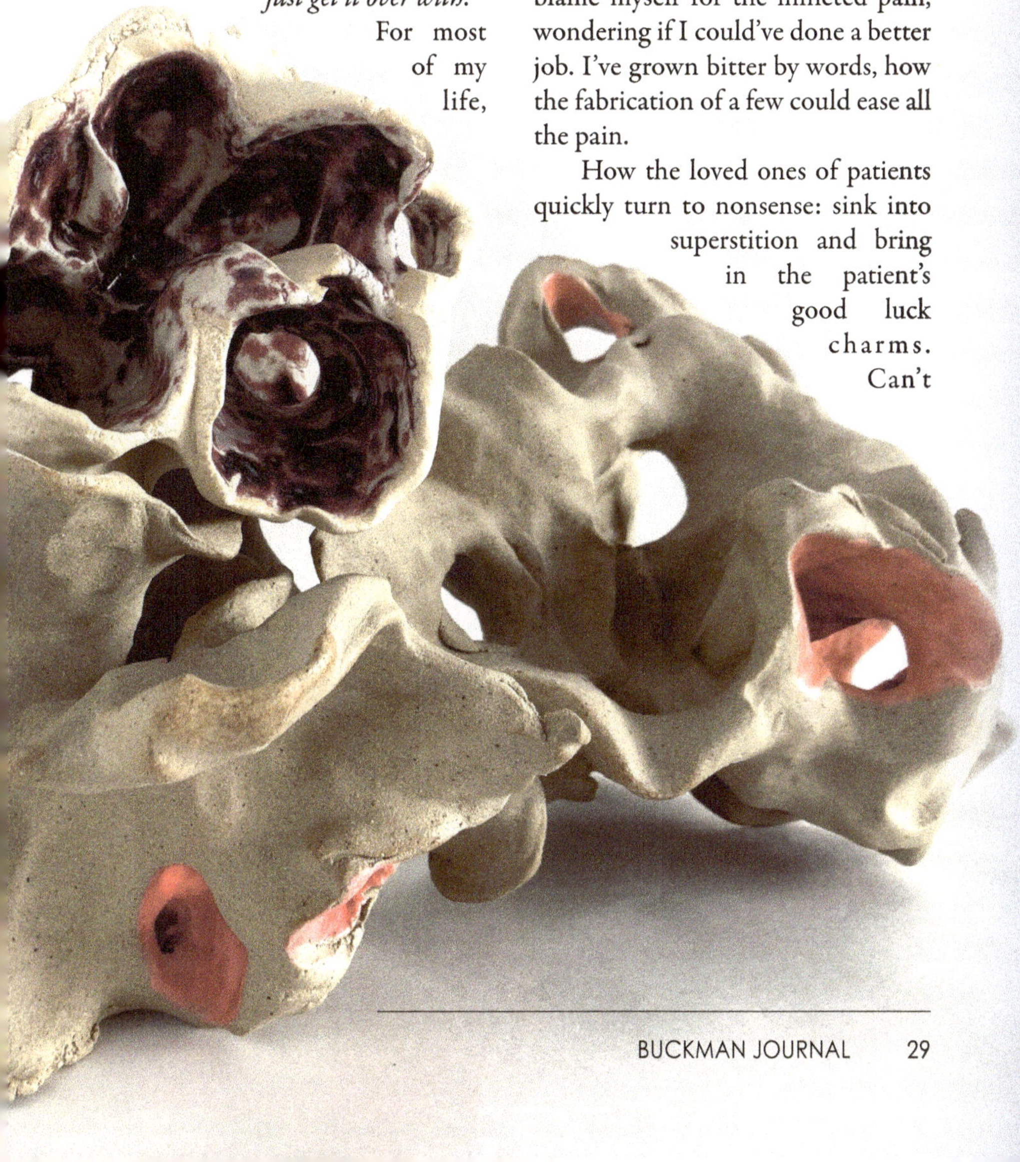

How the loved ones of patients quickly turn to nonsense: sink into superstition and bring in the patient's good luck charms. Can't find that one special thing? Favorite socks or beloved pieces of jewelry will have to do. Press those trembling hands together in prayer, plead for success in surgery. Tell stories about the patient's life: their job, anecdotes from childhood, hobbies, achievements. Say all this to an authority figure like God, or if he's not around a doctor will work, too.

"He has so much to live for," a mother once told me. Her son's heart merely murmured after she birthed him. Somehow, he'd grown up to be fifteen years old. No doctor told the mother to expect her son to live for as long as he did. She told me facts about her son emphatically, as if the stronger his narrative, the greater the chances for the surgery's success. He might live from the sheer force of his story's willpower. He needed a bypass surgery to create a path for the blood to flow around the blockage. I told the mother the same thing I told all my patients and their loved ones, "I'll try my best."

But some have no stories to tell and no longer hope for the best. Like that November a few years ago, I consulted a woman in her mid-fifties. It was a cold and dry autumn. She wore a brown cardigan and a steady hand. Gripped a blue pen and listed no Next of Kin as her point of contact. I assumed she forgot to answer the question, so I asked her if she knew any family members or partners I could list. But she was a divorcee and never had children. Both her parents were no longer alive. I left the question blank. I don't know if she survived because she was transferred

**"As I form slice a thin line the chamber's syntax molecules collapsing on**

to another doctor. Our fictions left to fate's hand.

In my first year of medical school, my father lost his job and my mother fell ill. That deadly, six-letter diagnosis: cancer. She was the kind of patient who denied everything. Said no to the pills and treatment. I asked to come home and she said no to that, too. Maybe she thought saying no would deny the cancer.

I consulted my roommate at the time, Rose, for advice. Rose's answers offered little clarity but we somehow shifted the conversation to whether we rose to the occasion or choked under pressure during important moments. "It depends," she said. "If academic validation is at stake, then I will rise." We are both daughters of parents who have traveled far from home. In Rose's little spare time, she also enjoys writing. We both write less for enjoyment and more as a survival tactic. She shares my quiet temperament, where most words hide inside her until she occasionally slices herself open onto the page. Still, on

**each sentence, I through, releasing contents of expanding and itself."**

the hierarchy of pains endured, we've been spared the suffering of our parents. We intricately operate on our sensitivities until we've picked out all the sadness, and only a clean sterile heart remains. Ironically, two months later, Rose ended up being the one who dropped out of school and left.

I called my mother and asked her again if I needed to come home. She scorned the idea and spat bitterly into the phone, pausing between syllables to hack out knots of phlegm: "If you give up on medical school, you are not my child."

I've always preferred my surroundings to be quiet. Must have started when I was younger, when I spent most days in silence. Since I knew too few words, I couldn't even stitch together the sentences children used to play make-believe. So I said nothing at all. The most I played was when I joined a game of tag on the school playground. I somehow always ended up as "it." The others shrieked when I ran towards them, a loud, painful cry that stopped my legs from running. My feet trampled over each other and I collapsed into the mulch. Everyone stayed away from me, unsure what to do about the blood running down my legs. The game dissolved, all my fault. The kids never let me play their games again.

I came home from school with two band-aids stuck crooked to my knees and hot, wet tears dripping down my eyes. The tearful weeping escalated into a full-on sob by the time I stepped into the house. Inside, I felt the safeness and freedom to throttle and crumble into my mother's arms. She did not care about the snot that dripped onto her blouse or the wetness dampening her body, because she knew she could not give her child the language or history or genetics to belong. At least she could hold onto these unbearable moments for me. She too struggled with belonging, and suffered the grief of losing a country. Instead, she could only offer the steady timbre of her heart. My ear pressed against her chest, I heard the blood of my mother's homeland pumping in and out like a promise.

I fainted during my first anatomy class. During dissection, we opened the stomach of a cadaver and I fell before I could say anything about my lightheadedness. After I regained consciousness, the campus nurse explained to me how my blood pressure likely dropped, my brain suddenly didn't receive enough blood, and I lost consciousness.

Later, I repeated what the nurse said likely happened to my mother in a phone call. My mother hates any rational explanation she cannot control. She immediately dismissed what the nurse said and asked if anyone else fainted in class. She reminded me how the other students used the anatomy lab to learn, how, in my little fainting spell, I lost an hour to acquire more knowledge. She told me I needed to be stronger, how I wasn't trying hard enough.

The grocery stores of Greensboro, where I grew up, pile towers of newspapers at the front entrance. The local news lists headlines about the clergy's inspirational work or instances of a firefighter saving a girl's kitten. Every week, my mother would grab a stack. She used the *Greensboro Daily* to clean our windows or to lay on the bathroom floor when she cut our hair.

Instead of the Greensboro papers, my mother read the news from Hebei, the province she grew up in. The words formed an illusion of closeness to her past. Because despite the 7,000 miles separating our little town from Hebei, her pulse belonged to the former neighborhoods she walked. Reminiscing on those schoolgirl days, she read about the gas leaks in the beloved restaurants of her past, policies implemented by Hebei executives on behalf of their citizens' futures. After dinner, she recited each of the headlines and then told stories pulled from her own life—she, the protagonist of a too-simple story, always sweet like a fairytale.

My attempts to abstract the form of my relationship to my mother always failed. I titled each piece of writing about us as "The Story of Me and My Mother." I wrote incessantly about why language breaks us apart, dissecting the psychology of my mother's brain, probing why she reacts how she does. Each time

I wrote the story, I would delude myself into believing I conquered our relationship, thinking we wouldn't ever bicker again. Inevitably, the fighting would happen and I'd try "The Story of Me and My Mother" again, rewriting us into something better.

Eventually, I gave up on the story because I filled each draft with what I now know are lies and nonsense. I began to believe there were no words to fully explain my relationship to my mother. I ran out of language; there were only so many pictures the stubborn words could paint, too small a supply of analogy to draw from.

To run away from the ambiguity of language, I look to the concrete facts in our bodies. I love my anatomy textbooks, appreciate the maps of our biology for directly addressing who we are. When I stare at a chart of circulatory pathways, I am baffled by blood's certainty, how each molecule knows precisely where to go next. Why wasn't anything else that perfect? After traveling its course throughout the body, blood remembers its path, circling back home to the heart.

"BLOOD FLOW CAN BE PREDICTED LIKE THE MOVEMENT OF MIGRATORY BIRDS, BUT WHO MIGHT BE ABLE TO MAP THE SHIFTS OF A FAMILY'S MIGRATION?"

No chart exists to predict what will happen next. Blood flow can be predicted like the movement of migratory birds, but who might be able to map the shifts of a family's migration? For my parents, no certain notion of home exists. Immigration broke home into two and two countries encompass its meaning. We brace ourselves for further breakage because who knows where we will go next. If the walls of an artery guide the magical intuition of blood, then my intuition is thin and fleeting, always hiding the truth. An invisible hand guides me to tools of destruction for the sake of repair, slicing long slivers in chests to recall the frankness of my body, the frailness of existence. My mother spoke English with a thick accent. It never bothered me, but the hefty-handedness of her language embarrassed her. From a young age, she had me respond to her text messages and emails. When we needed to call the electrician or the plumber, she handed me the phone. Her urgency for me to learn English was also for her own sake, as she raised the mouthpiece that would speak on her behalf.

I once mentioned I was writing a story to my mother. She didn't say

"We intricately sensitivities out

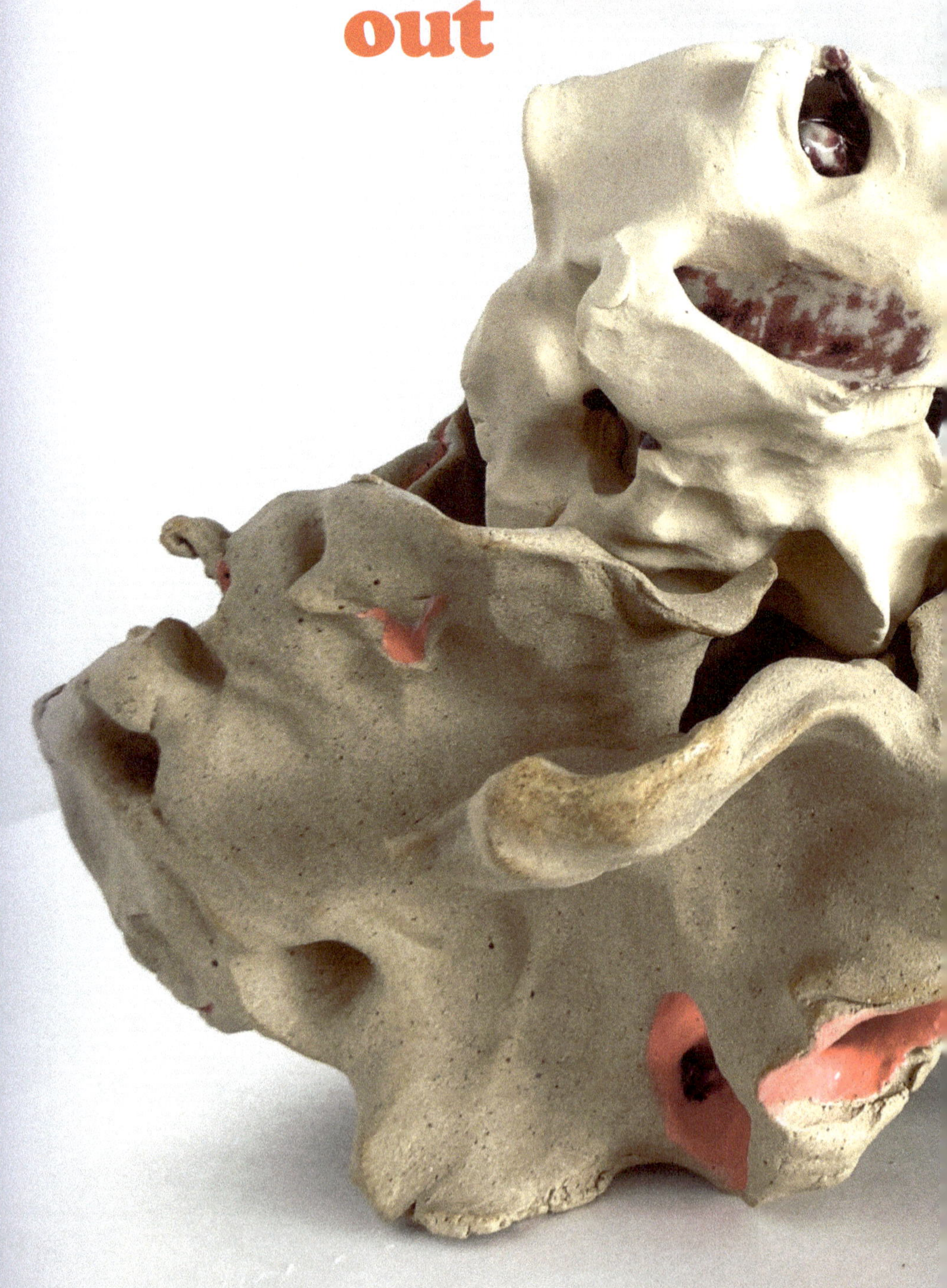

operate on our
until we've picked
all the sadness,
and only a clean
sterile heart
remains."

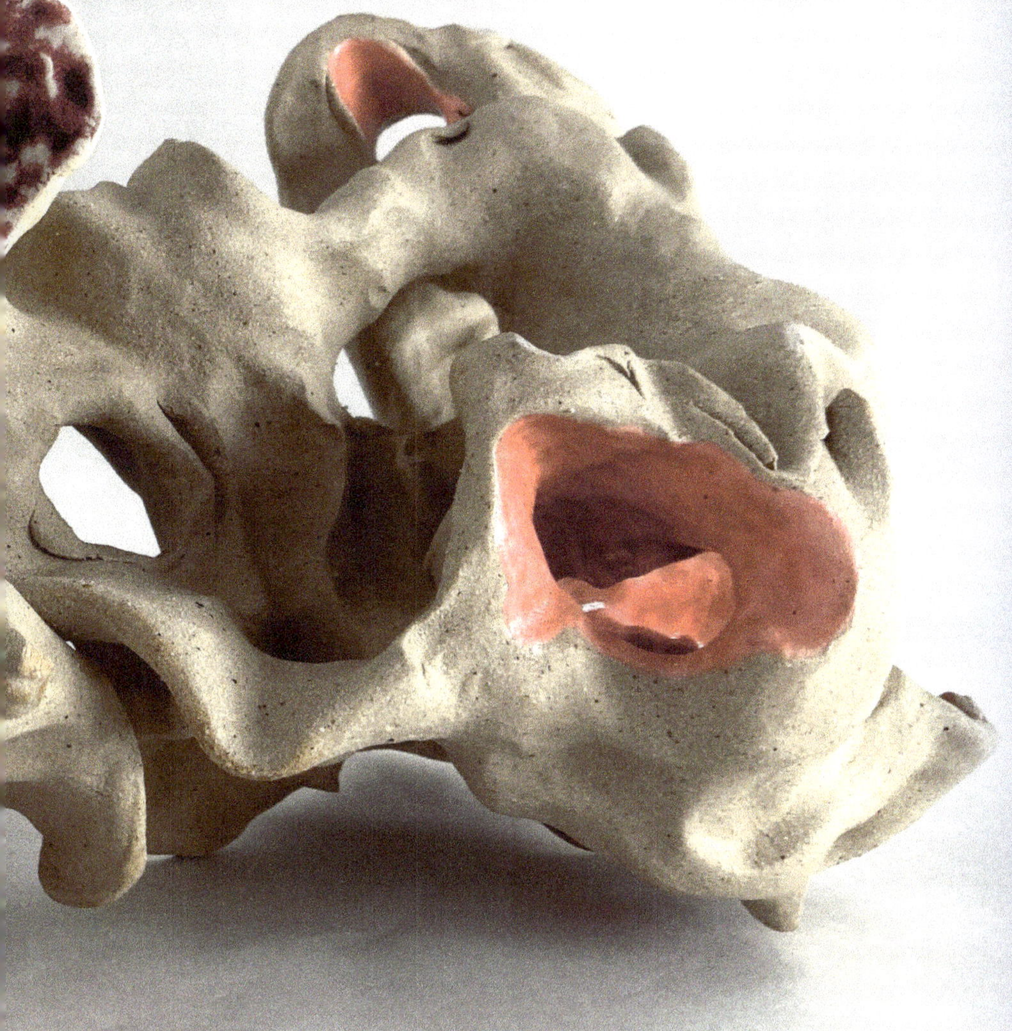

*SYNOVIA* (three)
STONEWARE, GLAZE, AND UNDERGLAZE

anything until I mentioned it had won a prize. She then beamed and told me "congratulations," but never asked to read it. Maybe she couldn't empathize with my compulsion towards language, or knew she wouldn't be able to read it without a struggle. She never knew the story was about her, or how this obsession with words started because of her.

But it wasn't like she understood much of my work as a medical student either. I didn't know how to simplify explanations about my surgeries in ways she might find interesting. Our mutual understanding suffered from the complexities of terminology and our dependencies on online dictionaries.

One of the worst fights between my mother and I occurred towards the end of her life. Her doctor recommended chemotherapy to kill the cancer cells looming in her body. My mother refused treatment and didn't tell her sisters in China about her illness. The refusal infuriated me as both her daughter and a future physician. I held onto the secret she hid from everyone else, but behind closed doors I couldn't hold it in. I screamed at her in English, she screamed back in Mandarin, neither able to hear each

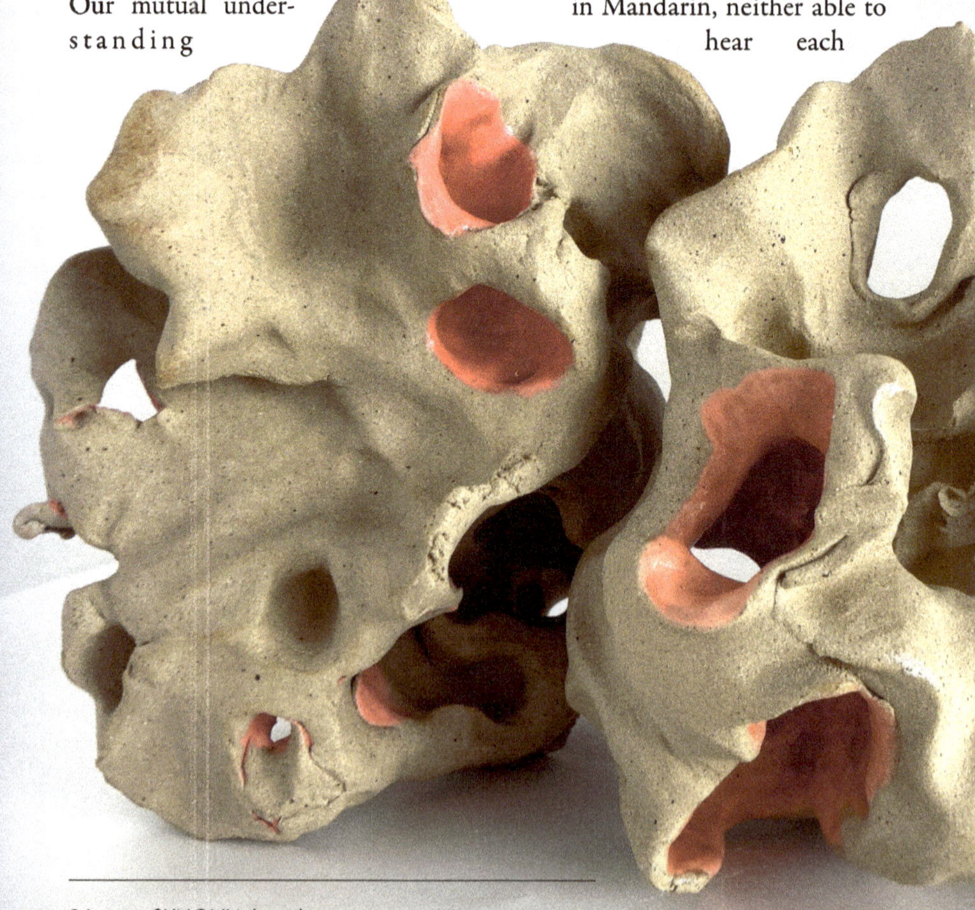

*SYNOVIA* (one)
STONEWARE, GLAZE, AND UNDERGLAZE

other's hurt. It eventually became easier to not say anything at all, and we settled on a three-month stalemate. Nobody said anything to anyone.

After some time, my father asked me to kill my stubbornness. My mother was slowly withering away and I needed to swallow my pride. Some ways of living will never be understood, like how my mother cannot fathom the joys given to me by electronic music and Tex-Mex. I don't get her either. We never spoke about death even when it was soon approaching. My mother considered it a taboo. When I asked her to explain her refusal to extend her life, she hushed me. We would never speak of it.

After my mother received her diagnosis, many of the doctors wondered if she couldn't understand what they told her. They expected a sad reaction or any reaction at all. But my mother acted as if someone merely told her the time. She smiled politely, thanked them, then drove home.

My mother never treated the loss of her own mother with any strong feelings. "Grandma died," she said one day, and that was it. She felt none of that inertia that comes with grief. For a long time, I couldn't understand why she rejected the treatment and said no to everything. But my mother understood more clearly than me how nothing is guaranteed once you're born, besides death.

When a patient dies during surgery, their body is sewn back up before it goes to the morgue. Upon clinical death, the body loses its human quality. The skin pales, blood vessels no longer move, the heartbeat terminates.

Sometimes, a medical resident will do the re-sewing, like I did during my residency years. The first time I sewed back together a chest incision, the body hadn't fully lost its softness. I could see the deep caverns leading to the heart, the pink hue of the skin. I nearly apologized for my intrusion. As the patient rested in utter stillness, I peeked where the patient had been cut up to see what color it was inside: a glossy deep red, not blue at all, and streaked with dark, plum lines.

My mother died ten days before the Lunar New Year. If she lived for ten more days, she would have entered the year of her Chinese zodiac, the dog. My father delivered the news of my mother's death to each of her sisters scattered across the provinces of China. Her three sisters decided they would fly to America. Perhaps for the funeral, perhaps out of curiosity for the life she kept hidden.

My mother avoided sharing her life to her sisters. On calls, my mother would mention me and how my studies were going, and that'd be all. She worried that if her sisters saw the cluttered house and the icy-blue eyes and the cheese on the plain food, they wouldn't understand why she stayed here for forty-two years. In this American period of her life, my mother never invited her sisters to visit. And so they never came. Perhaps she was still figuring out why she stayed, too.

Before my aunts arrived, my father and I dug through all her old things to clean out space for my aunts to sleep. We found the mail she collected from over a year ago, mountains of Hebei newspapers, textbooks from my father's college days, the Junie B. Jones books I read to learn English. The room adjacent to my parent's bedroom stored all the clothes my mother didn't know what to do with. She stacked boxes full of my baby clothes to the ceiling. I should have told her to let some things go, get rid of the clothes, tidy up the place. But I knew my menopausal mother. With a daughter in her thirties, she would protest in earnest: "*No, no, maybe we need it.*"

**"I OWE MY DESIRE FOR DISSECTION TO MY MOTHER BECAUSE A PART OF ME ALWAYS WANTED TO KNOW...**

**...HER A LITTLE BETTER. I WANTED TO LEARN HOW TO OPEN SOMEONE TO SEE ALL THEIR BROKEN PARTS."**

My aunts arrived, and so did an urge to hoard all my mother's clothes and things. I wanted my aunts to tell me all the pieces of information I didn't know about my mother, but when I mustered out a question about their upbringing, they responded with brief answers. In part due to my limitations in Mandarin, but maybe my aunts share my mother's inclinations against words.

In the evening, I curled my body into one of my old pink baby shirts and wept into the soft cloth. Smelled like the old soap she liked to use. I moved all her things, all that useless crap that suddenly seemed perfect, into my childhood bedroom. Only a small, cramped path remained free to tiptoe from the door to the bed. I didn't mind because I finally agreed with my mother: we needed to keep these things. Finally, I relinquished my own expression of love to practice hers, love voiced not as language on the page, but through all the things one owns.

The body retains memory in ways the brain fails. February 6th used to mean nothing but now it's the day my mother died. I fear how someday, it won't mean anything again. Just another day. But then I heard a story about a woman who threw up every January 5th. She began to notice the pattern the third year in a row when she realized January 5th was the day of her miscarriage. In another story, I learned how the heart might function for memory storage. People with heart transplants supposedly experience the memories of the heart's donor. Say I do forget she died on February 6th, fuck the memory of the mind, I'll have my body to remember her. My heart, and the hearts of her sisters, all beating the same blood that won't forget.

My mother understood happiness in momentary pleasures. She preferred to spend her money on useless junk because of the dopamine hit to the brain. American pleasures trained her like Pavlov's dog to follow these transitory exchanges of coin for contentment. Eventually, a home can be filled entirely with little mementos of happiness. I think she would've said she lived a good life.

I never pressed her to kill these habits because to restrict her intake of junk and clutter would mean killing the little remains of who she really was. She lived and died surrounded by the piles of envelopes, magazines, and receipts. On her last day alive, she watched QVC with one hand on her phone and the other on a tall glass of cranberry juice. On her lap was the silver wrappings of a dozen Hershey's Kisses. What use is a doctor when the end is impending?

In my eulogy, I intrnote-oduced myself as my mother's daughter, reminding my aunts and father we share the same blood. I told the story of my mother's stubborn heart, how it beckoned her towards this country and this family.

Our skin encases blood and organs, a boundary we can't transcend unless we cut ourselves apart. I owe my desire for dissection to my mother because a part of me always wanted to know her a little better. I wanted to learn how to open someone to see all their broken parts. I never got to slice my heart and then my mother's in such a literal way, to see proof that our hearts beat the same and shared the same blood. Now her heart had stopped beating and the blood no longer flowed. That's all death was.

Of course, I did not say this in front of my aunts or the rest of the funeral party. Instead, each of my organs said it quietly to all the other organs in the room. I don't even remember what I actually said that day but the body always remembers. We live on, all of our organs remembering how they belong to one another. ✿

**Creative Non-fiction by**
**Rich Perin**

# Minneapolis

I was going to check out Paisley Park, Prince's secluded estate just outside Minneapolis. But it's no longer a house of magic, the conjurer is gone, and now it's a well-ushered tourist attraction with pricey, time-restricted tickets for a tour that ends with the standard exit through the gift shop.

I've never been one to glean local character and vibe from tourist attractions. They're mostly generic products of Americapitalism, contrived and shined hard, insisting must-see status.

Minneapolis is fine by me. It has defining characteristics that make it unique, everything from its signature dish (the Juicy Lucy), the strong union history, and a bunch of world class art galleries and museums.

But the site of horror and tragedy, George Perry Floyd Square, resonated most with me when I visited. It is not ideal to relate a city to one of its low points, and Minneapolis is obviously more than the lynching of George Floyd. But the response from the Minneapolis' Powderhorn neighborhood—more specifically the blocks around 38th Street and Chicago Avenue where the square is located—is noteworthy for its bravery and defiance.

I wasn't planning to visit the site but while in Minneapolis I learned it was the fifth anniversary of Floyd's death. The video of a prone and handcuffed Floyd slowly asphyxiating while a white police officer kneels on his neck was a turning point in the national consciousness regarding the Black Lives Matter movement. All Americans could watch the entire ugly ten-minute ordeal and recognize nothing else but injustice. The truth laid bare—minorities still faced a different set of laws even after a Black president.

George Perry Floyd Square is

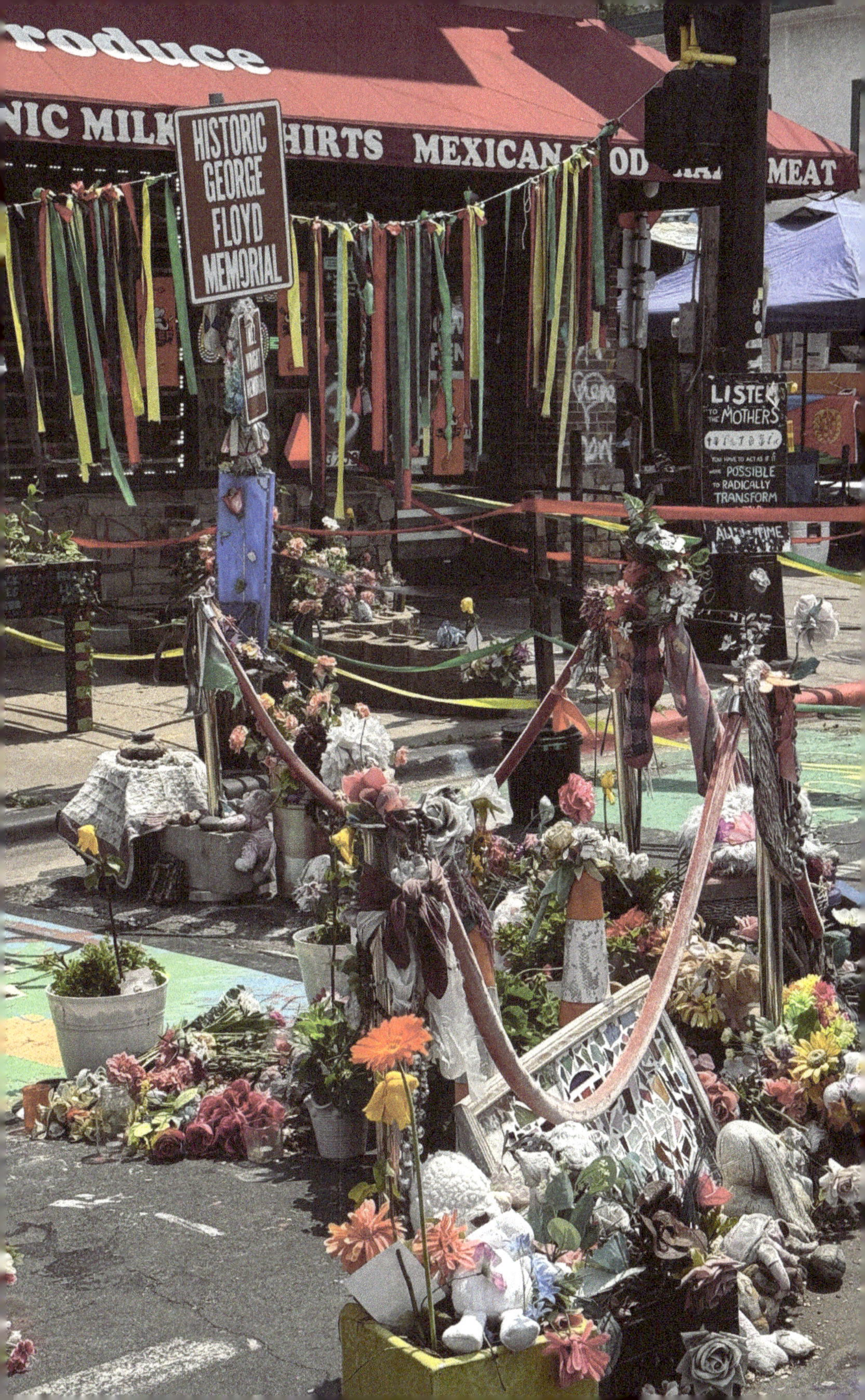
roduce
NIC MILK
HIRTS
MEXICAN
MEAT
HISTORIC GEORGE FLOYD MEMORIAL
LISTEN TO THE MOTHERS
POSSIBLE
RADICALLY
TRANSFORM

a memorial unlike others, not designed by celebrated architects or worked over by planning committees, and never twisted to conform to a city-permitted process. It's unfiltered. The people that live in the community are the creators.

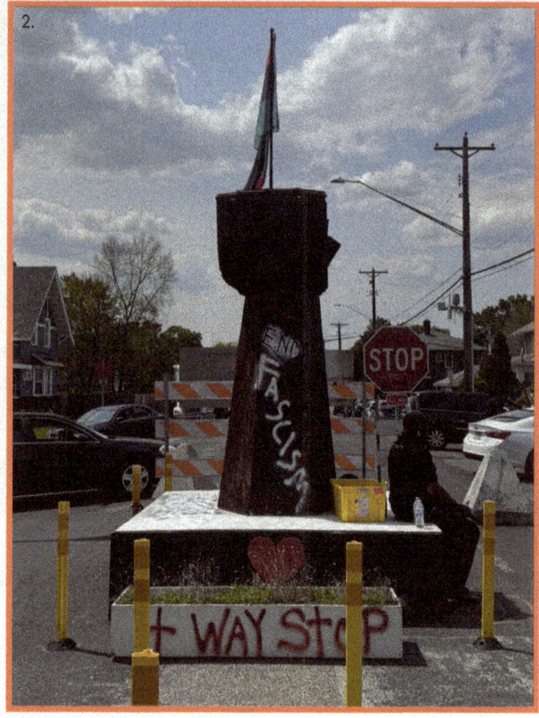


The neighborhood is solidly working class and has been so for generations. After the initial Scandinavian immigrants left in the 1920s, East 38th Street became the epicenter of Black culture and entrepreneurship in Minneapolis. Since the 1980s, Black enterprise spread elsewhere, Brown folk settled in, and these days it is a blended neighborhood, the abundance of diversity immediately apparent—faces of all races, people of all ages.

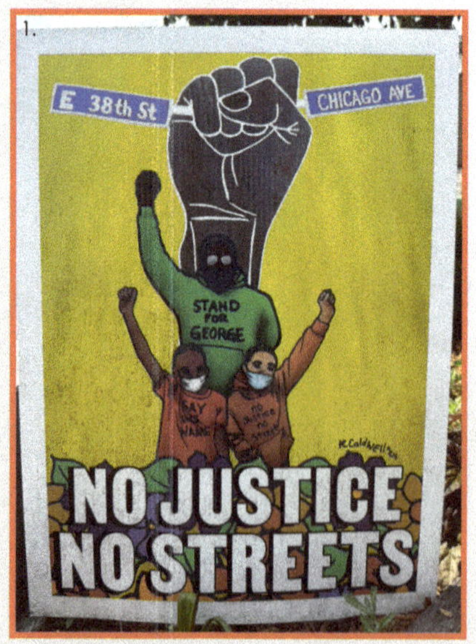


At the intersection of 38th and Chicago, in the middle of the street, rises an iron statue of a giant fist, about ten feet in height, made by little-known artist Jerome Powell Karis. It's called *Black Power*. A small garden in the form of a traffic island encircles the statue, tended and maintained by volunteers.

Steps away, outside the convenience store where Floyd was killed, flowers, wreaths, messages, and prayers carve their space out of the street, an altar for people to step forward, bow heads, and reflect.

The convenience store itself, whose clerk called police suspecting Floyd passed a counterfeit twenty-dollar note (the clerk later expressed great remorse calling authorities, considering how the



1. THE NEW PROTEST SLOGAN; 2. THE ORIGINAL PLYWOOD BLACK POWER SCULPTURE IS LOCATED A BLOCK FROM GEORGE FLOYD SQUARE.

responding police officers reacted), is now called Unity Foods. It is a community hub, one of those odd neighborhood stores that dabble in things besides convenience items, a genuine one-stop shop, something that the rigidity of national chain franchises aren't able to replicate. Phone repairs, a deli, international money transfers, a small restaurant with a few tables, and other side hustles play out in Unity Foods.

Outside the store, spray-painted on Chicago Avenue, are names of racial violence victims. Ahmaud Arbery, Sandra Bland, Trayvon Martin, name after name after another, a list that spans several blocks. It's a reminder of the easy slide into seeing such deaths as statistics. The names on the street confront normalization. The length of the roll call is horribly long.

Other small, independent businesses line the avenue. A BBQ joint, mom-and-pop restaurants, art galleries, cafes, a laundromat, and others eke out a living. Workers and proprietors welcome with smiles and *good days*. The neighborhood has suffered a great wound, but there's a refusal to be defined by the trauma. Instead, energy is channeled into making the community they want for *themselves*. Aside from proclaiming and con-

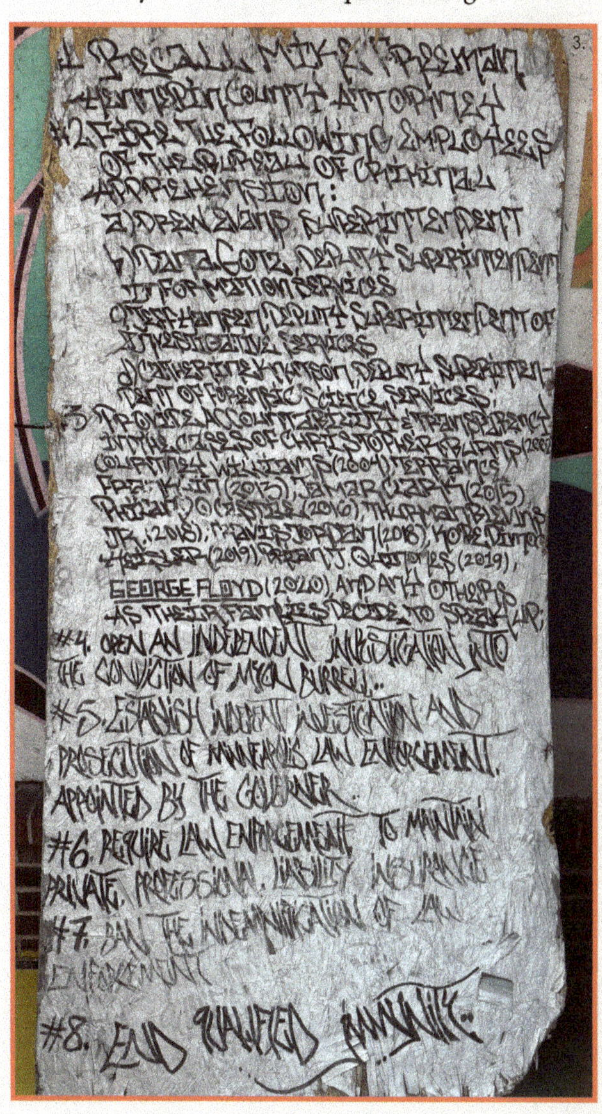


3. A PANEL FROM THE ORIGINAL 24 DEMANDS MADE BY THE COMMUNITY AND PROTESTERS FROM 2020 ARE STILL DISPLAYED AT GEORGE FLOYD SQUARE. SOME HAVE BEEN MET, SOME REMAIN UNANSWERED.

"The neighborhood has suffered a great wound, but there's a refusal not to be defined by the trauma. Instead, energy is channelled into making the community they want *themselves*."

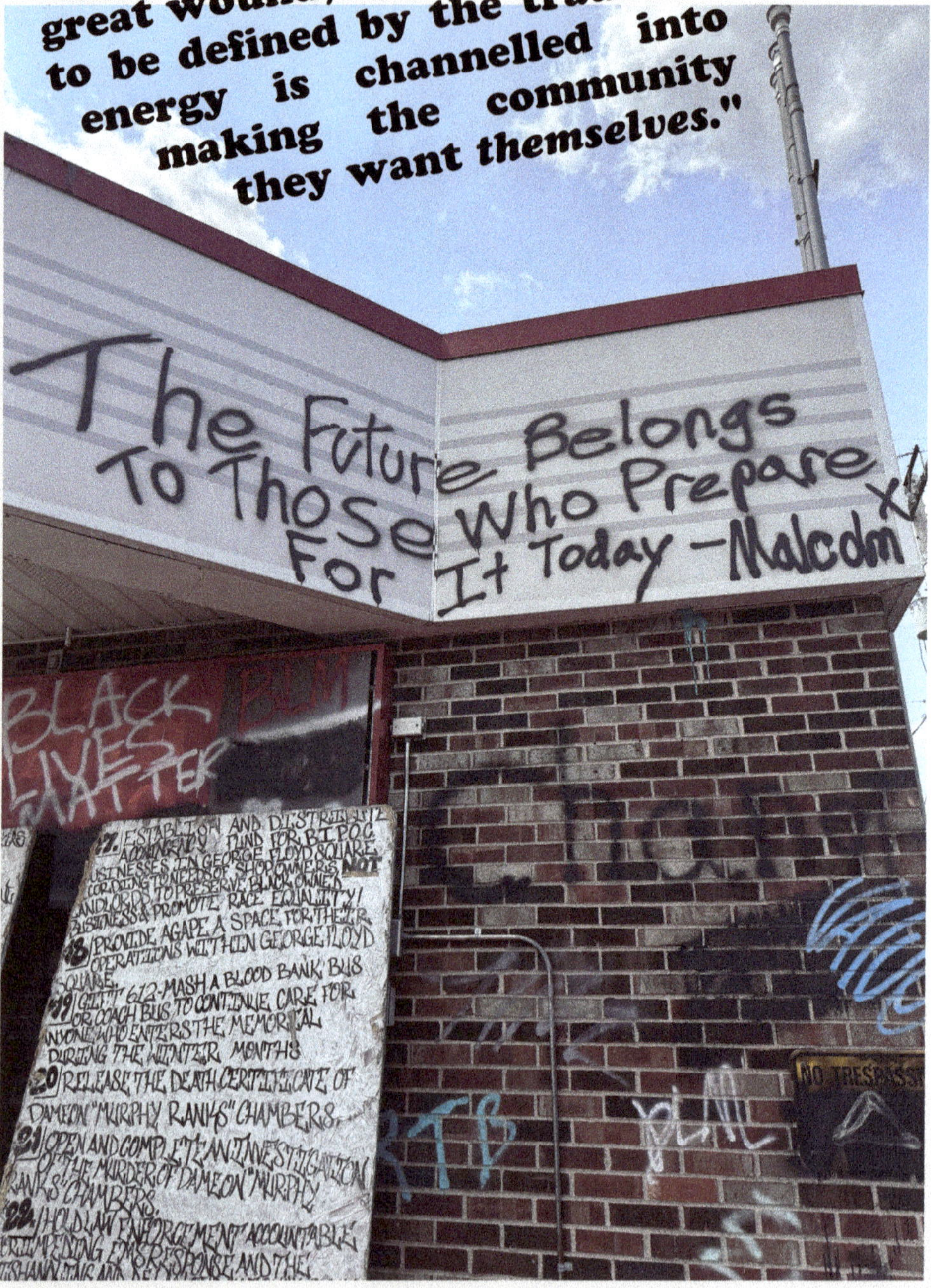

structing George Floyd Square, locals made chairs and benches for public seating, and converted a Metro Transit bus shelter into a free clothing store. The abandoned gas station transformed into a community meeting and dining space, *"The People's Way."*

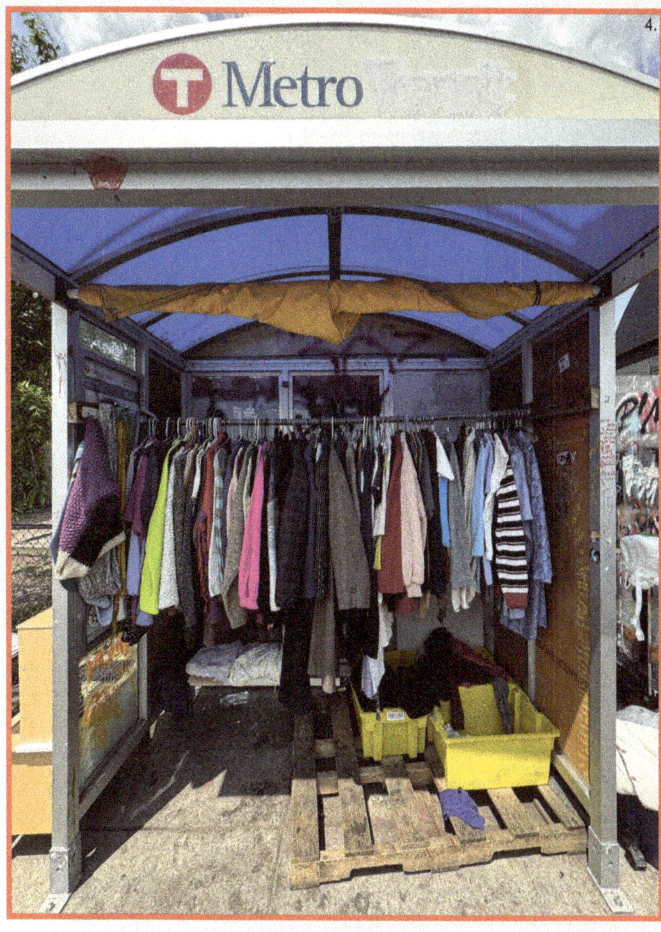


When I was there, before the flowers for Floyd outside Unity Foods, people stepped forward and made soapbox speeches about how the murder had shaped them, their anguish, what they wanted to change. Someone that I presumed a local addressed those gathered, and after a few words about hopes, yelled the first line of the familiar call-and-response protest chant: "NO JUSTICE...." The crowd responded, "NO PEACE." But the local shook her head, and corrected the crowd, letting them know WE have moved on from the line. "It's No Justice, No *Streets*," she says, explaining that she's had enough, if the police and city and system are a source of injustice, then those institutions don't deserve the streets.

The people are the authority. There may be some amount of naivete, but they are fully aware of the hard work needed to manifest their hopes. They don't know how long it will take but even in these early days of transformation there is crystallization, something is forming. ✿

4. METRO TRANSIT BUS SHELTER REPURPOSED INTO FREE CLOTHING STORE.

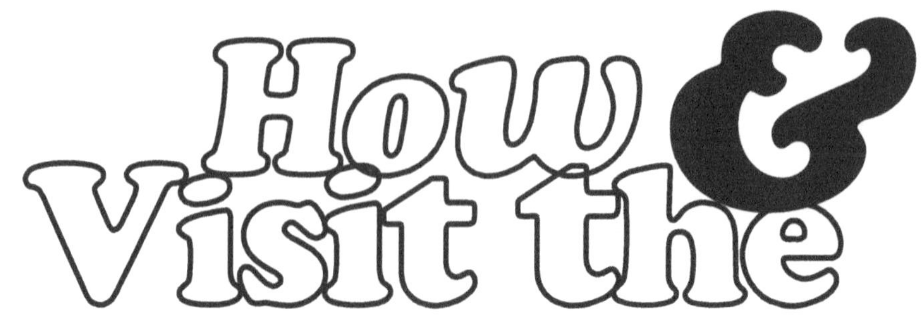


We live closely with other people in the city. We bring animals close to the city and group them together in the zoo so we can observe them. My family must go to the zoo to see the animals. I have to round them up and prepare their bodies. They have to defecate. They have to put on clothes, they have to eat. They will need to groom themselves. And then I must get them in the car.

They will run out of the house and to the car and I will order them to confine themselves within the car in their restraints, which they can fasten themselves. And they are able to escape these restraints, their purpose is to reduce the chance that parts of the car will pierce and crush and destroy their bodies. So they must be restrained when they're in the car. While they're confined, they're still able to strike each other, and perform further biological functions such as eating, or releasing mucus from their bodies.

These are the preparations that we must make so that we can leave the house to go to the zoo. Many have already been performed for this objective. The car has previously been fueled. The car has been maintained and repaired. A bond has been purchased in case I murder someone or destroy something with the car. It's very easy to use the car to destroy other things. So I have contributed money into a pool that will then pay anyone who gets destroyed by one of its participants. As a group we can engage in a rate of killing and destruction and the cost is distributed among us over the year. And there's a large amount of infrastructure that enables the car to be a machine that can transport us to the zoo. There are roads that have been paid for, traffic control devices, police officers.

And then we drive to the zoo. We have to pay a fee to leave our car next to the zoo on a large paved area where many cars can be stored. We walk through that area, between the other cars, and we arrive at the zoo. The zoo is a large plot of land which houses several enclosures that cage the animals inside them, animals that wouldn't be living there normally.

***Essay by***
**Karl Anderson**

# Why We Zoo

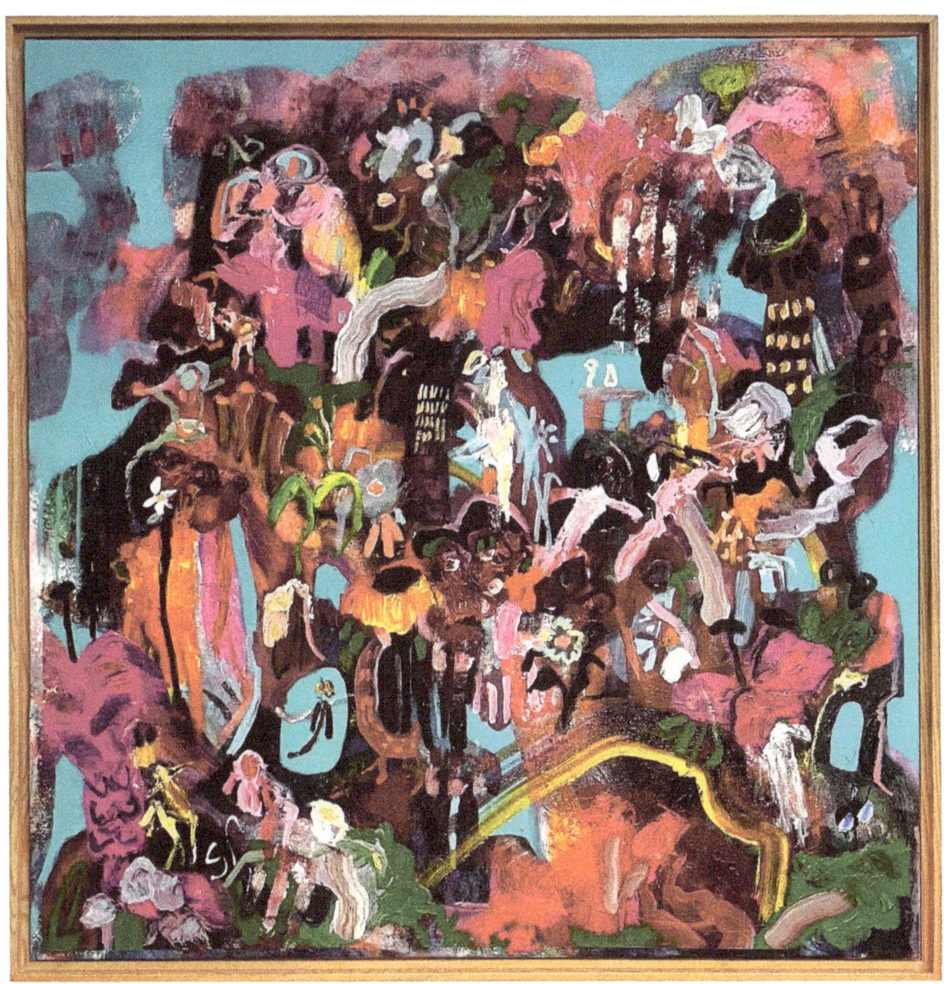

## Painting by Kristen Diederich

*The Angels Pool Their Tips at Night No.1*
ACRYLIC ON CANVAS

They are caged in that way for our viewing convenience. They are fed and maintained. Their bodily needs are usually taken care of, allowing enough of a population to survive until our arrival. The animals are bred for the zoo or are abducted from their environments to be brought here and placed in these cages so we may observe them. Their habitats are more symbols than simulations. For example, there is a tiny swath of savanna for lions to live in, but not enough to do savanna-like activities in. The lions cannot kill. They cannot roam. They cannot gaze into the distance.

These creatures conduct their lives in a mechanized way. The lions are tossed chunks of meat they have not hunted. The lions are not acting as a lion would in a pride of lions. Their actions represent a larger set of possible natural activities

**"It lets us feel that we are doing something...**

which they are not able to undergo. Their piss and shit is removed, and their dead bodies. They receive medical treatment and are allowed to live as a captive representation of what would be their normal lives. And we walk around and observe them. There are other items in the zoo to represent these fuller lives that we are imagining when we see them. There are sculptures. There are artificial signs of animal life, footprints, scat, scratches, claw marks, and other indicators of animal activities in the area. These indicators are representations. They are made of metal or stone or plastic. They have no odor. They are not tactile.

This zoo, of course, is on a large plot of land that has been set aside for this activity. There are workers. There are people cleaning, sweeping, picking up trash. There are people frying up hamburgers and hot dogs and french fries, and refilling the pump ketchup dispensers. There is lots of very cheerful and encouraging signage, especially for the food items that can be purchased. Colorful and whimsical signs. And we spend several hours there having these experiences. Walking on the paved paths.

There are the primate enclosures. Monkeys and chimpanzees and apes can lounge and groom each other and climb on things. Although mainly they are sitting around and they appear to be trying to figure out what they can do next. They may experience excitement about the possibilities. And all of this is in the context of this land that has been set up for the zoo activities, and the vast infrastructure around that. The taxes, the bonds, the wages.

We wander from location to location, observing the animals. In the course of one day, we will see polar bears and elephants very close to each other. And this gives us wonder. This gives us enrichment. This allows us to imagine a life with animals and plants in it that are interacting. An ecosystem, a biosphere. It lets us feel that we are doing something. Striving. Putting food on the table. Locking doors to keep predators out.

And then eventually we are done. The decision that it is time to go needs to be made wisely. If it is delayed too long, there will be anger, and frustration, and weariness. We have to leave just before we want to. We have to leave when we wish we could stay longer, because if we wait until after we should have left, there will be punishment, unpleasant noises, harsh language, violence. This is how we interact within these constraints. There will be consequences to try and

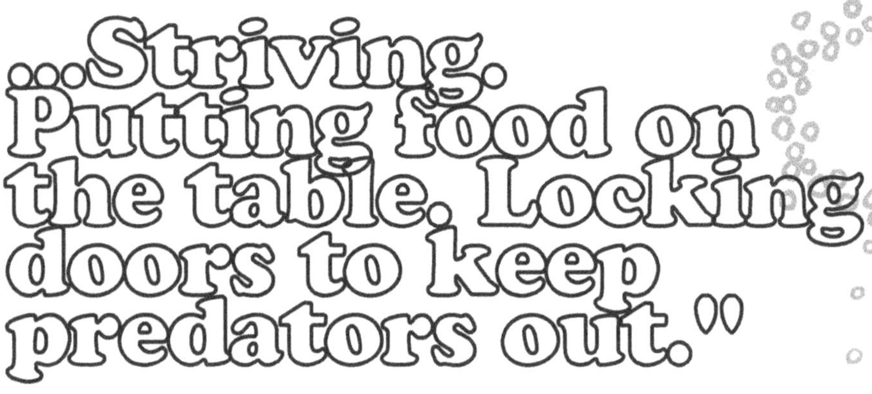


steer future behavior into a pattern that is more accommodating for our bodies. Our needs must be met within the forms that have been established to enable this closeness. Toilet use must be encouraged. Many aspects must be predicted to avoid unpleasant outcomes.

But the decision will happen and we will walk through the zoo gates, and back through the area with all the cars in it, and we will get back in the car and into our restraints. I will drive the car back to the house and we will be freed from the restraints and we will have done it. We will have observed exotic life. We will feel that we have not been lounging around, considering what to do next, unenthusiastic about the possibilities. We will be fulfilled. There will have been a reason for this day. ✿

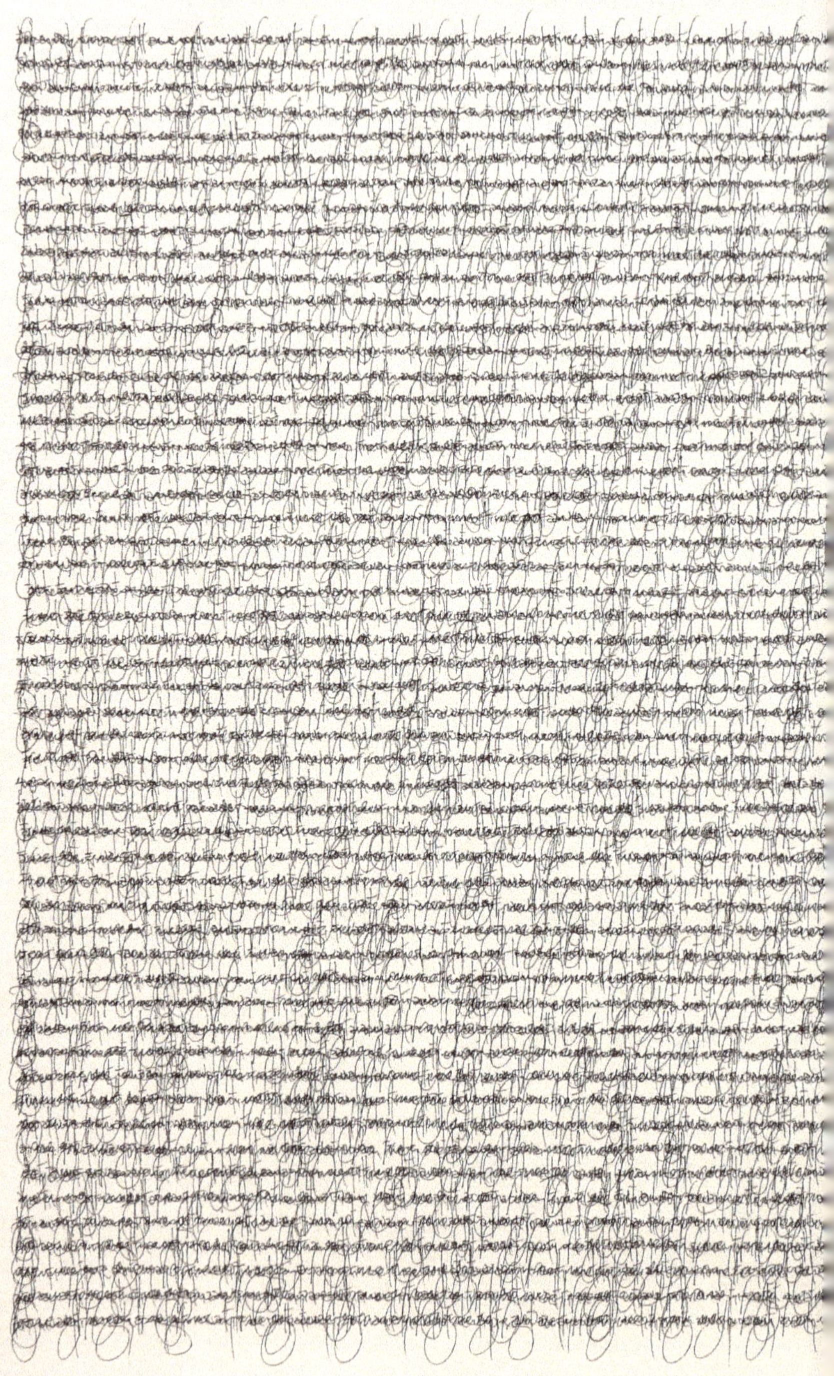

**Time Got Away From Me**
INK ON PAPER

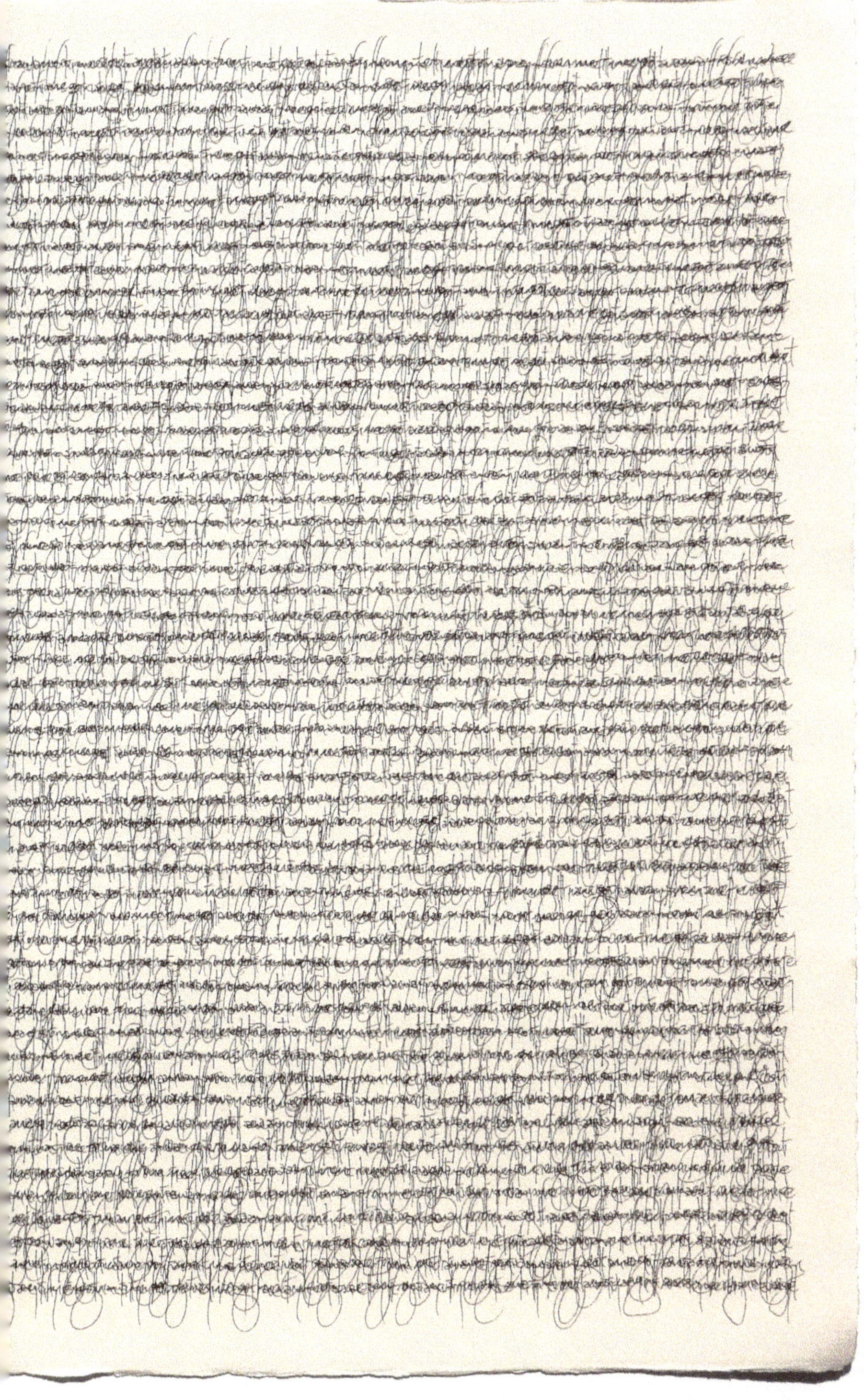

**_Drawing by Ocean_**

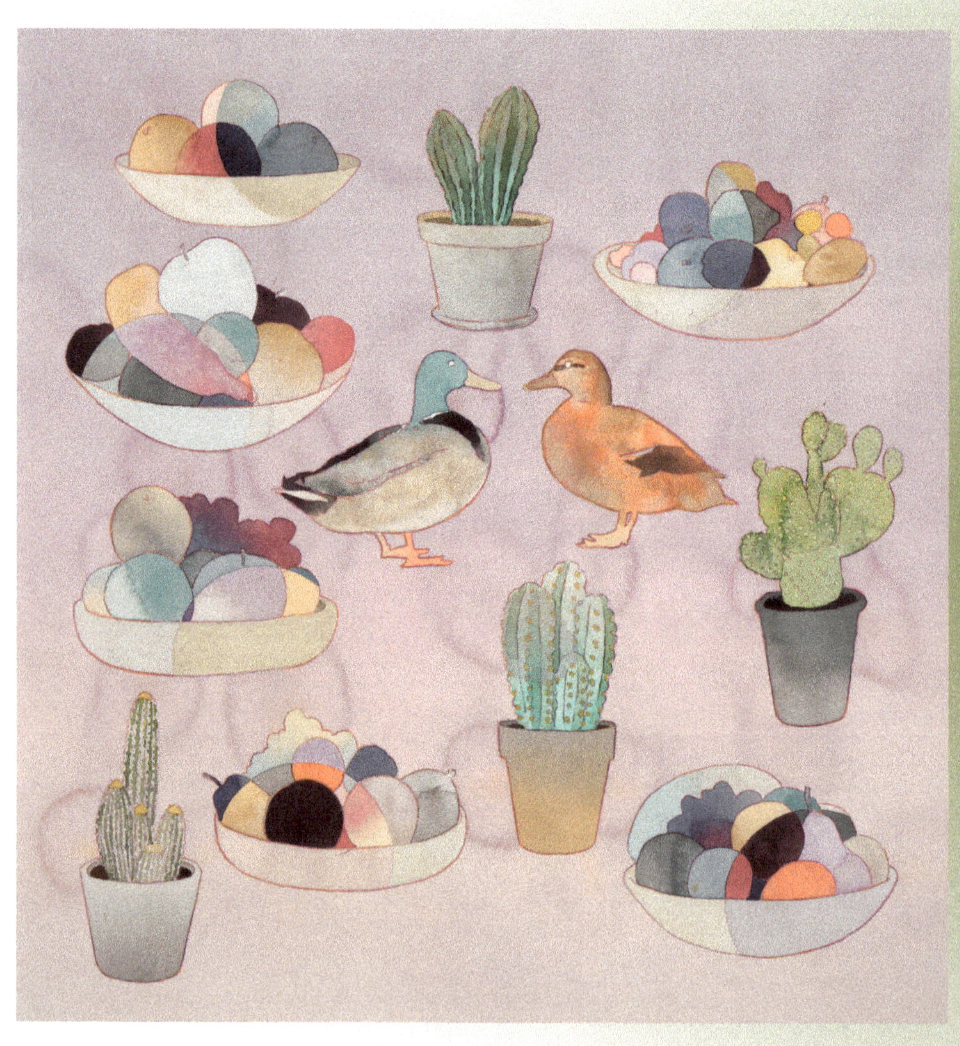

## *Painting by*
## Dan Gluibizzi



*Love*
WATERCOLOR, ACRYLIC, GOUACHE, AND COLORED PENCILS ON PAPER

## *Baby's First Joke*

Because it's good to talk to your baby, I talked to mine all the time. It was just the two of us day-in and day-out. They say it doesn't matter what you say, so I said just about anything, whatever came to my sleep-deprived mind. She was bound to have good language skills.

I was consistent too. She had this egg-shaped shaker, a music maker, and whenever we shook that thing, I'd say, "Shake-shake-shake, shake-shake-shake, shake your booty." Of course, I also demonstrated.

Or sometimes I'd say to her, "Guess what chicken butt," apropos of nothing.

She was about a year old when, one day, as I was busy doing something, as per usual, at the kitchen counter, she says to me in all seriousness, "Guess what?"

I stopped doing. I looked at her in all seriousness.

"Duck booty," she said.

**_Creative Non-fiction by Dana Cera_**

## *Asshole*

My dog and I attended a friend's backyard party. A handsome married stranger observed me sipping gin from my flask, which I kept in my purse at the bottom of the porch stairs. I saw him see me through the wooden banister slats, all the way across the yard.

Later, washing my hands at the kitchen sink, I heard my dog outside, his incessant, rhythmic, loud bark, which he deploys whenever I leave him for more than a few minutes, more so now that he's going blind and can't take the stairs.

"Asshole!" I said out loud.

I turned to go, and there stood the handsome married man in the doorway.

"Oh," I said, by way of explanation. "I was talking to my dog."



*Bounty*
WATERCOLOR, ACRYLIC, GOUACHE, AND COLORED PENCILS ON PAPER

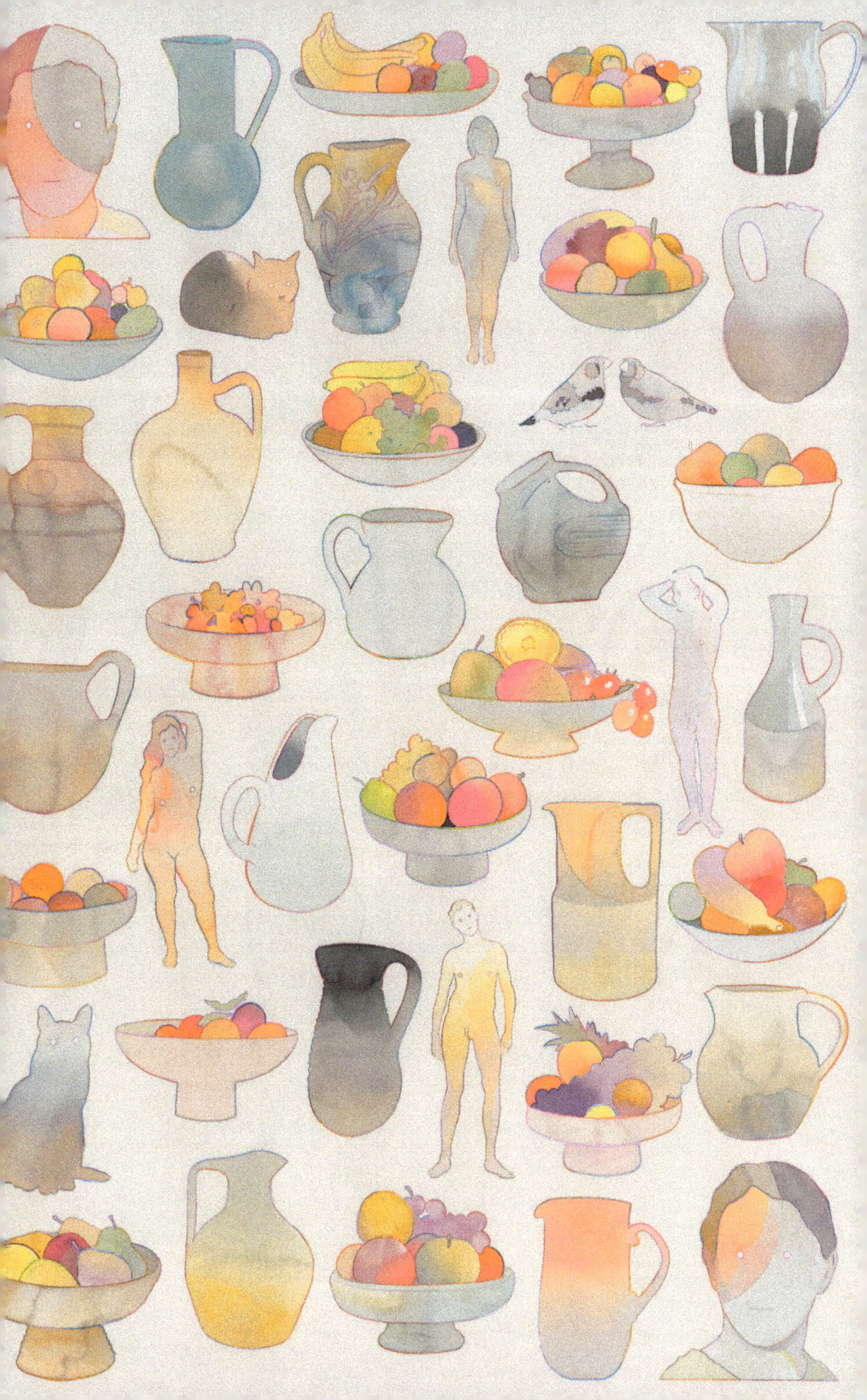

## *A Single Woman Goes to an Annual Solstice Party for the Last Time*

The golden retriever sniffed my crotch when I entered the house, a mansion in the West Hills. Just put a snout in there and left it. A man said to me, "Because he can." I said nothing. His wife would leave the party early. He would ask the hostess for my email address.

My friend, the hostess, took my coat, then my arm. She wanted me to meet *that divorced English writer* she'd told me about at last year's solstice party, who couldn't make it that time because his plane couldn't leave London due to weather.

My friend was excited. "He's still divorced," she said under her breath, leading me towards him.

He was tall, thin, with a balding head and a handsome face. In the dining room, around the table laden with food and decoration, he asked, as he chewed, "So, what do you do?"

"I manage a toy store," I said.

Welp. That was the end of that conversation. A tall woman wearing a backless top asked him to help her get a beverage and they talked the rest of the evening. Years later, he would message me on a dating site, not recognizing me. I would call off the date we made, confessing that we'd already met.

Another man talked to me for ages, until I met his wife. These two would sing a holiday duet within the hour.

After spilling a shocking amount of red wine then cleaning it up, I wandered sweaty into the living room and spent the rest of the evening in conversation with the hostess's father, a physics professor twice my age, pushing ninety, his torso permanently bent forward as though he'd pored over too many books. I had known his wife, dead a decade already.

Maybe it was the wine, or the exhaustion of managing a toy store at Christmas, or my singleness singled out all night long, but I cried when telling my friend's father about my most recent relationship that had ended abruptly, on Valentine's Day no less. It was a trifle compared to losing the love of one's life after a lifetime together. Mine was just a three-month mindfuck with a malignant narcissist thirteen years younger than me. But the professor listened, cheering me—I thought—by telling me about the three women he was currently seeing. One liked to talk, one liked to go to dinner, and one liked to have sex.

Another man asked me if my friend's father was my husband. I would take offense.

At the end of the evening, my friend asked me if I wouldn't mind taking her father home, since he lived on the east side too.

He would ask if I wanted to come inside.

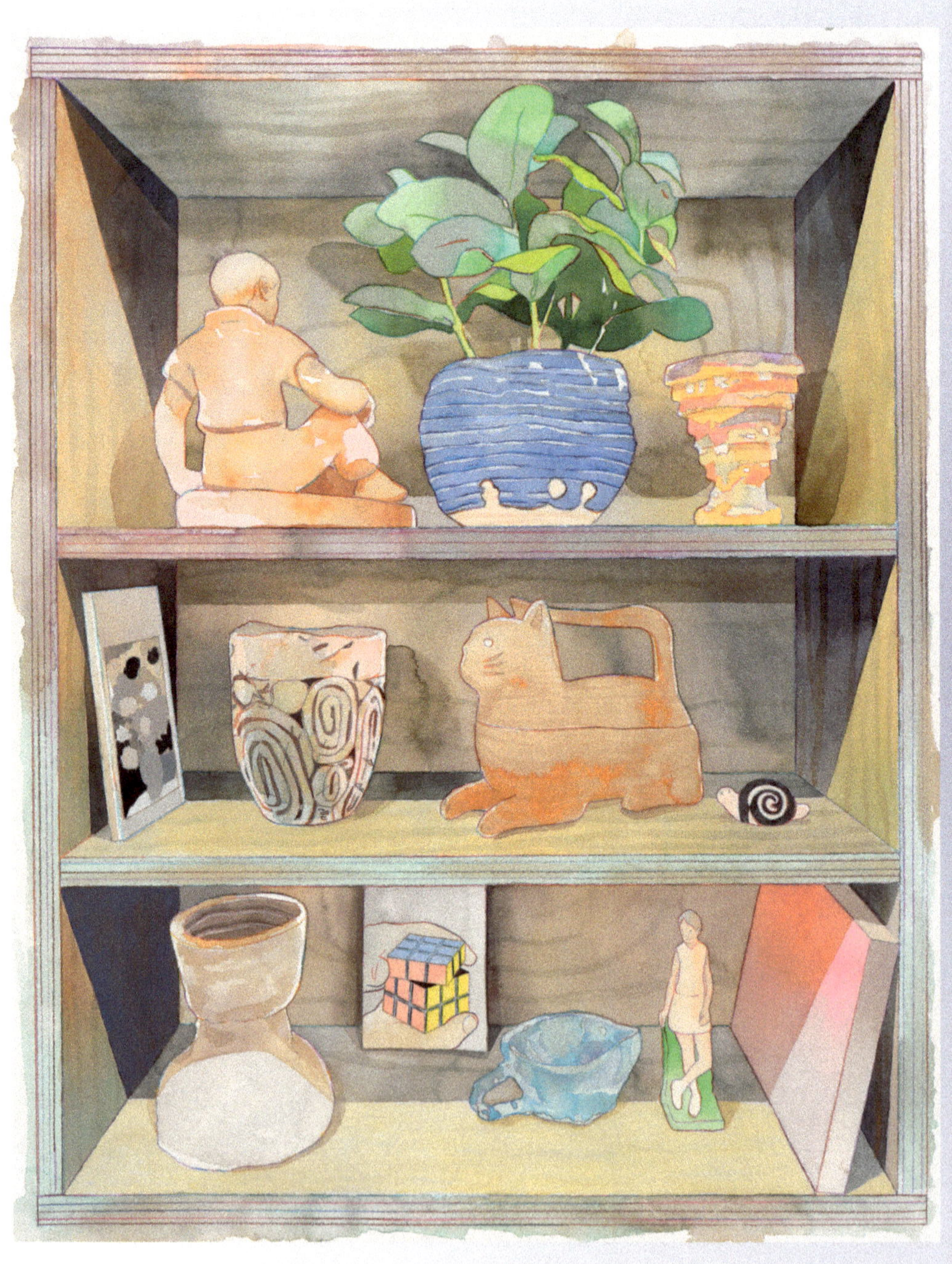



*Solution*
WATERCOLOR, ACRYLIC, GOUACHE, AND COLORED PENCILS ON PAPER

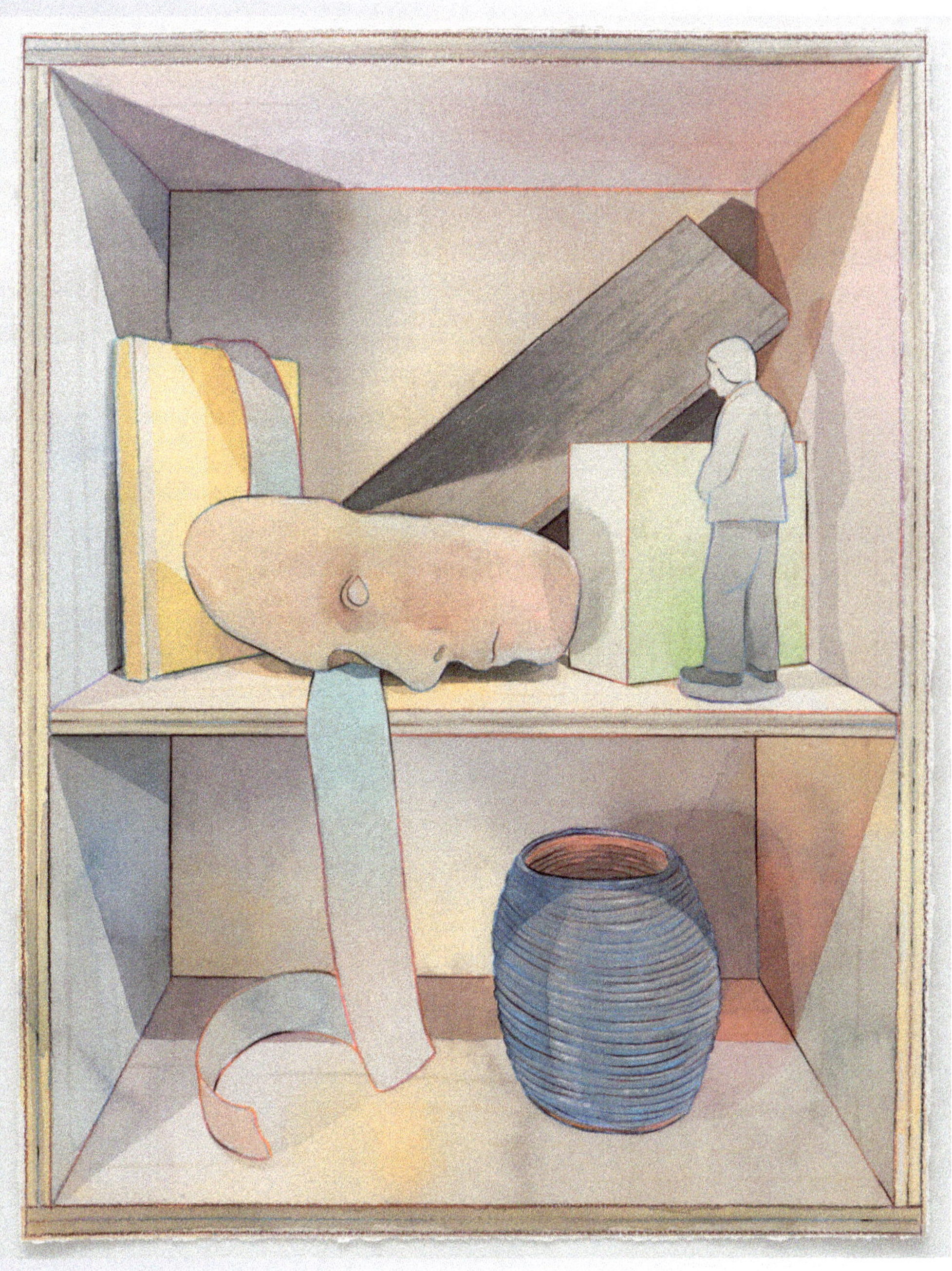

*Flow*
WATERCOLOR, ACRYLIC, GOUACHE, AND COLORED PENCILS ON PAPER

# Appetite

*Armillaria moves beneath the leaf mold, sending its fungal finger-threads through earth rot-rich with lignin and decay. It is a silent network, older than the tallest tree. The veins of life. No one has mapped its reach. It takes what it's given, making a meal of all fallen things. A wet cradle for the soft collapse of everything. At the tree line, he squats, tilts his neck to trace the arc of shelf mushrooms climbing a yew's spine: white moon-fruit purling among the sun's spider-lines. One breaks beneath his finger, its tissue part marrow, part sponge. Was it here you buried her? Softening enough to be digested. He listens for the carbon and nitrogen moving underground, exchanged in chemical language. Pit and pulp. Every body is a soft fruit for the soil to open. Some animal impulse in him, like a larva chewing through meat, compels him to lie belly-down and stretched out, as if to let the hyphae learn his shape. He thinks about his instruments. He thinks about all the things nature has made that man cannot imitate: lignin, chitin, keratin. He thinks about skin. A beetle clicks beneath his boot. The boundary between self and soil begins to blur. He kneels among many little moons. God is nearby, mouth open, waiting.*

**Fiction by**
**Rowan Tate**

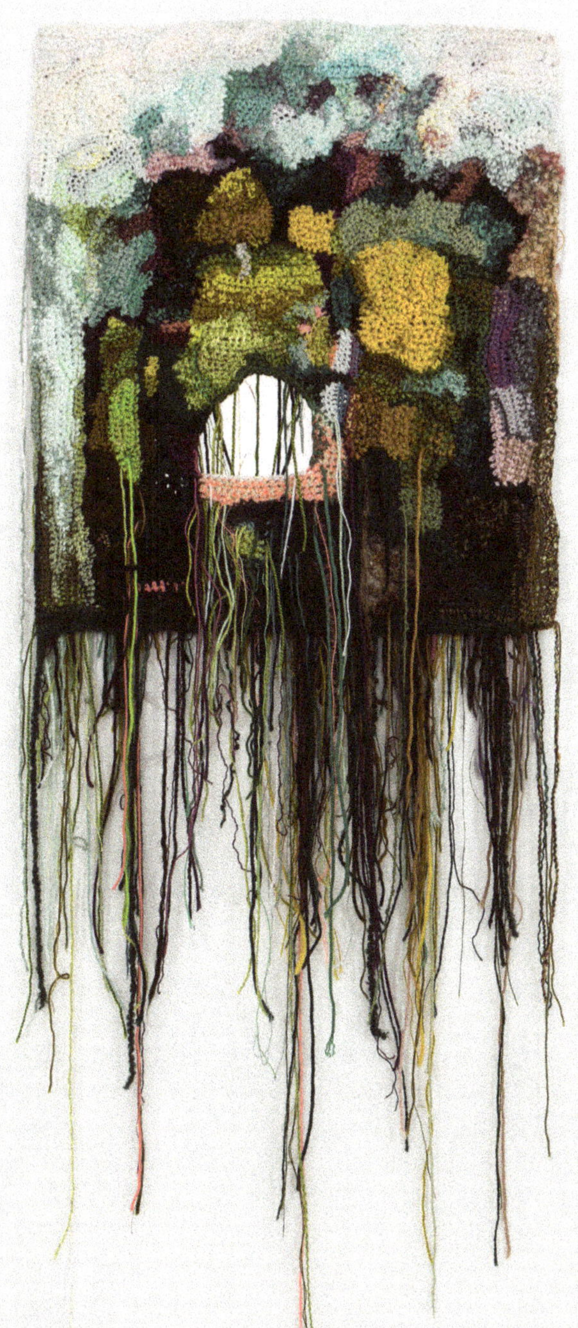

# Textile by Jo Hamilton

*Dear Green Hollow*
CROCHETED MIXED YARN AND MIRROR

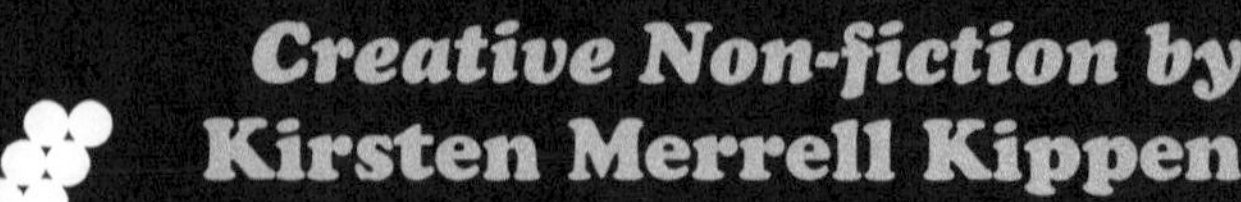

Creative Non-fiction by Kirsten Merrell Kippen

# The White Peacock

The rhododendrons are nearly done for the year. They carpet the path around our house, magenta smearing into the concrete. My children make soup, pouring petals and rainwater into an old pewter teapot that lives in our yard. They stir it with a stick, adding fern fronds, chalk dust, and pinecones. “We’ve made fruit soup! Come taste it!” they crow. If Mom were here, she would be asking about all the ingredients, suggesting new concoctions. It would absorb the afternoon.

Instead, Mom is in an RV park in the Santa Cruz mountains where she recently moved to be closer to my brother. Twice a week during supervised visitations with his kids, Mom spins up a world of love with craft projects and copious amounts of Annie’s mac and cheese, pretending for the kids that everything is fine.

Then she drives back to her RV until the next visit. I glumly picture her life shrinking to the size of the RV. I imagine her surrounded by retirees with gaudy lawn ornaments and handheld chihuahuas.

“It’s not so bad!” she texts. “There’s a white peacock who roams the RV park’s paths!” She tells me the peacock has a long, feathered tail, a bobbing head, ancient dinosaur eyes. Locals feed him; he is a symbol of the town’s resilience after surviving a recent wildfire. “His name is Albert! We walk together every morning,” she texts. I scrunch up my face, trying to picture it. Maybe I have it all wrong, maybe things aren’t so bad down there. I imagine Albert and Mom swapping secrets. What would they say?

Two pink envelopes arrive in the mail with Mom’s familiar handwriting: one for each daughter, addressed using their full names. The first card shows a panda in a pink hat eating a pink donut. It’s no one’s birthday, but Mom has been sending cards more regularly. It’s been four months, the longest she’s ever been away from the girls. Mom writes: “I am sitting here sipping coffee but not eating a pink donut. I'm also listening to see if I can hear the white peacock. He is such a pretty bird but has a very obnoxious and loud call. He does seem to like being under the redwoods."

I learn that white peacocks are usually not albino, but leucistic: they're born with a genetic condition that strips them of pigment and inhibits melanin from depositing in their feathers. I learn that white peacocks symbolize cleansing, purification, and spiritual awakening. It's the second time this year I have encountered a leucistic bird. I hunger for omens, for patterns that add up to something.

Last winter, as we crunch-stepped through the snow during a December visit to Alaska, Dad told me all the local birders were in a tizzy over a white raven sighting. It settled for a few months between two dive bars in Spenard and was seen with pizza in its mouth, its feathers the color of midday on winter solstice. Later I found out the leucistic raven had its own personal paparazzo, a former police detective who had snapped over 10,000 photos of the unlikely celebrity. I felt my brain flip, seeing the familiar shape of a raven but the wrong color. Something about this seemed correct to me in this backwards year. A Yup'ik prophecy says that when you see a white raven, humanity is shifting toward peace. But raven is also a trickster.

**"I hunger for omens, for patterns that add up to something."**

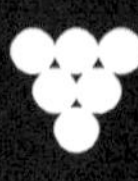

Mom sends the girls another letter a month later, this time including a few downy white feathers that float immediately, landing under the couch. "I made sure he didn't need them anymore."

She texts me videos of the peacock. I want to feel awe, I really do. I want to believe in a magical undercurrent of beings supporting our family, shapeshifting into whatever we most need. We were raised to believe that hard times only make families stronger. But I'm worn out after a day of carpools, playdates, bickering over dinner, endless bedtime requests. I delete the videos without watching them.

Days go by. We shapeshift ourselves: baby cheeks morph into set jaws of independence. We get a new puppy, swap berries and eggs with neighbors, make a thousand choices every day about how to live, how to be. Dusty soccer games and late-night popsicles shift to long days of school. The rhododendrons set new buds. Nature runs its course, sometimes resilient, sometimes not. And when I hear, six months later, that Albert the white peacock has been killed by a mountain lion, it does not feel like a sign. ✿

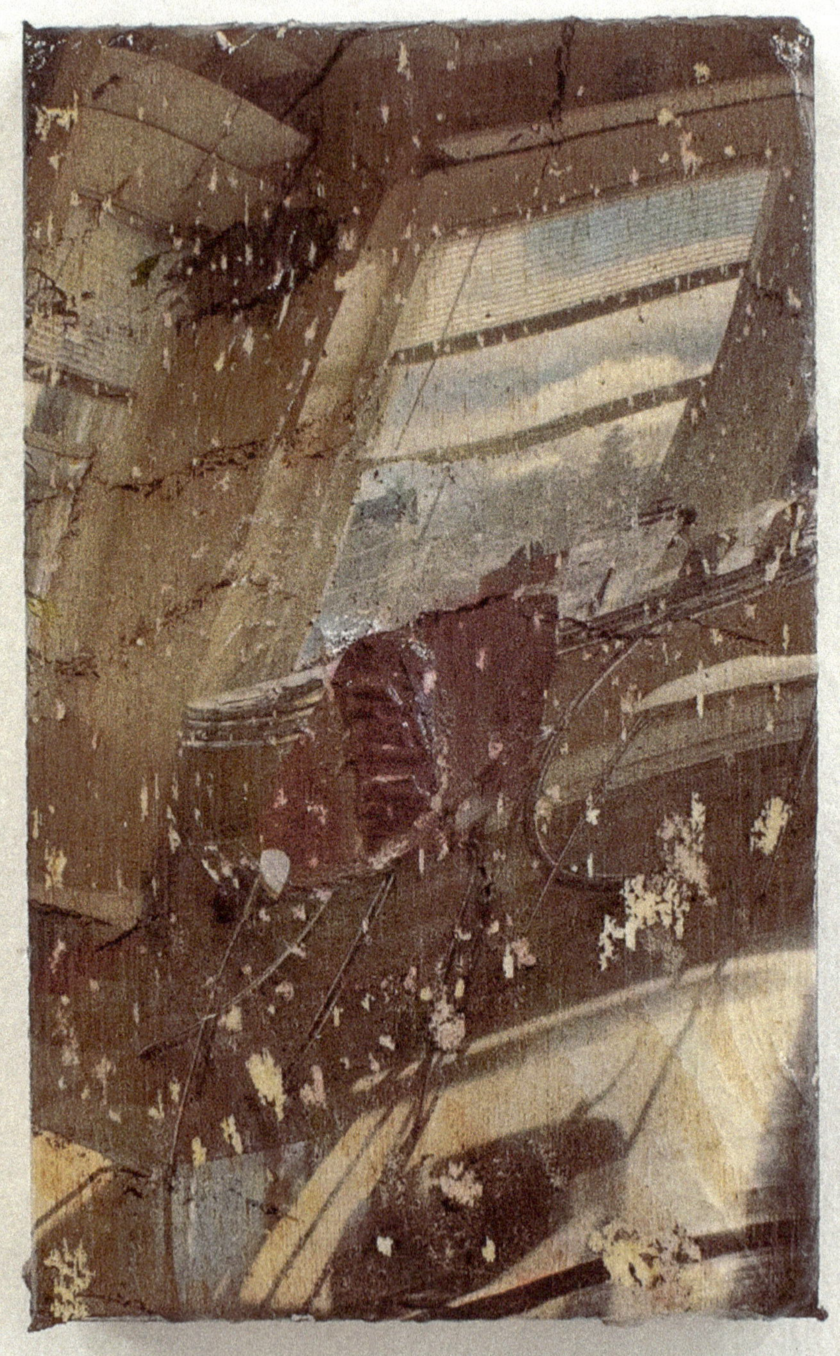

*Mixed Media by*
**Nicholas Moler-Gallardo**

# Simone

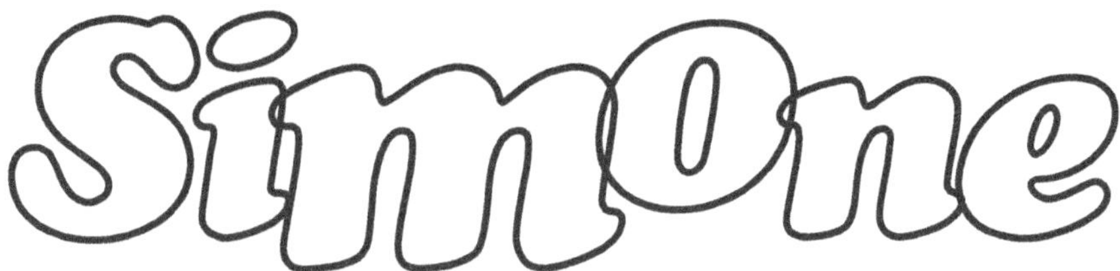

She wiped front to back like everyone else, performed elaborate evening skincare routines of algorithmic active ingredients: snail mucin, menstrual blood, and cheeto dust, took public transportation daily without so much as a traumatic stress response when passengers assailed her, and, if late, she ordered a personal driver without wincing at the price. What else to say other than she was born into, and internally organized by, a quality of detachment.

Human instinct was not impressed upon her. Despite having been conceived in the same city where she lived, she knew its arteries no better than a tourist. Maps and mapping technology overwhelmed her nervous system. Their aesthetically displeasing design choked her retinas. As others point North without magnetic consultation, having had their poles calibrated young, she insisted on pointing down—always down—without registering the fixed posture of her finger. Onlookers would say she walked through the city as if she followed the scent of a situation about to kick off. Where her finger tensed, a situation soon followed. The simple fact was that she had no sense of direction whatsoever. Every time she arrived, it was due to luck.

It was not appropriate, her attire. She wore lingerie in public: leather riding boots, crisp cotton boxers, and a retired sports jersey, which belonged to a young boy whom she had no relation to. Her dress was oriented sartorially two months ahead of the times. But prediction was not something she did. In fact, her capacity for immediate foresight was so terrible it made her an unlawful liability on the road. She could not drive. Her preemi-

**Fiction by**
**Kaya Noteboom**

*Distorted Time Cluster, Passing Light*
HYDROGRAPHIC FILM ON PLASTER

nent sense of style was instead ruled by an internal digital clock-face, the timing of which elided her conscious awareness. She did not believe in the risky choices of her clothes. She did not know they were risks and therefore did not think it was a choice. If it had been a midsized sedan instead of an outfit, she would have been dead.

She would have died despite all the best efforts by her parents. As a child, she had a sleeping chamber that her caregivers protected

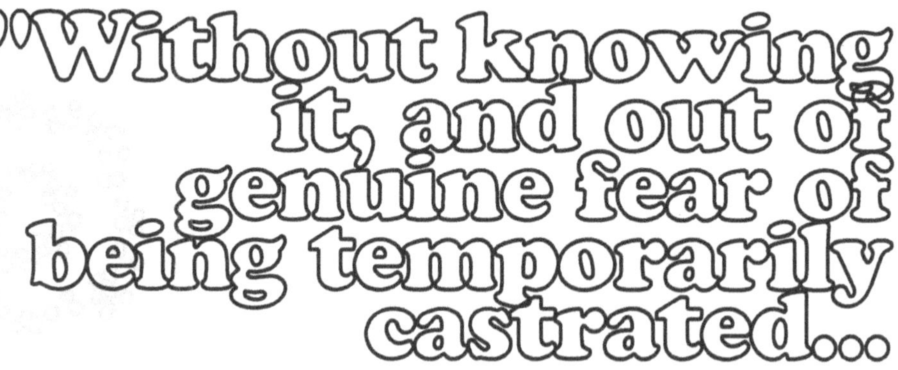


like the Alamo. With organic combed-cotton sheets, weighted blankets, and a fascist dominion over the evening hours of their young nextdoor neighbors, her mother and father devoted themselves, body and soul, to her sleeping-self. For all their efforts, it did not matter. She fell asleep easily under far less favorable conditions. She awoke well-rested and even-tempered. At night, she did not dream.

Her eyes remained open in daylight. On the way to work, from the inside of the tube train or self-driving car service, she saw ordinary atrocities. Demolition equipment appeared in the parking lot of a historic elevator factory, then disappeared with the building. Downtown a man in a neon safety vest lowered the front of his jeans to piss into the back of a moving truck. The commercial ships did not dock at the harbor as they usually did. Their crated passengers did not unload onto the shore. It did not comfort, nor excite her to see these atrocities. Each one arrived without expectation. She simply waved it onward like a somnambulant pedestrian hovering on the edge of a sidewalk. The atrocities came and went, sure as the coming day. Her senses were attuned to a perpetual present that never lowered its hackles. She kept these atrocities to herself.

Men of a certain age and profession saw her and saw a dollar sign. The men were in their late forties to early sixties. They held directorial positions in the decentralized administrative structures of liberal institutions. They were hungry men with beautiful ex-wives and lonely men whose ex-wives were their best friends. They met her in typical ways she could have seen coming if she had any foresight at all.

Soft power advanced her. In her presence, these men interpreted her magnetism as unusual competence. What they had actually perceived was their libidinal attraction to her—a fact their institutions would not tolerate. Without knowing it, and out of genuine fear of being temporarily castrated, they translated their sexual desire through a fine mesh. Their institutions would

**...they translated their sexual desire through a fine mesh."**

accept an assessment of competence. It was false on their part but not without a grain of truth. Though her intelligence was middling she made decisions without pause or deliberation. She was capable as only flagrantly disinterested people could be.

This is how she was selected to take over a semi-national nonprofit. It was a position she was unqualified to hold and yet the organization scaled up gracefully under her blasé leadership. Her uniform did not change. She wore her lingerie.

The nonprofit processed hostage negotiations. After her first month, she steered the nation into a peacetime. During this period she gave herself to volatile relaxation. She stopped coming to the office. Instead, she called in from home where she pruned for hours in her tub and marshalled ants into urns of honey. Tired of baths, she circled back to the office. Now she bound her breasts in cellophane and brought flat soda in her coffee thermos until the purple band of an ocular migraine began to cinch her vision. She had to loosen her breasts. A detached wisdom returned to her. A wisdom sharp as the sword sheathed in adhesive wings between her buttcheeks. Ten months into peacetime, a new war started.

She had grown anxious about war, peacetime, and the attachments she did not have. She made an excuse to leave the office for an indefinite lunch break, though no one supervised her productivity. The train stop was seven blocks away. Her house was fourteen.

A screw rocked between passengers' feet on the feces speckled floor. It was packed. Men of a certain age and profession. School children. Unschooled women from warring nations. Toddlers and babies, the children of spring. Contemplative dogs of some sizes. She stood gripping one of the yellow hand-rungs. It was two stops from her house when a stranger got on. There was nothing about him anyone would surmise. Her interest piqued for no traceable reason other than a new smell meeting air.

What resulted within the small nation of passengers over the next train stops was a war she could not negotiate. There would be few survivors.

Among the brutalized she sensed a whimpering need for a certain future. She made something up, saying to no one in particular:

> *Empathy is barbaric. Kindness is evil. Love is a mechanism of terror. Saints, if they exist among us, grace us with attention, always insufficient, always bereft before understanding, all ears with no mouth. You will live some part of your life without hands. You will form a soul marriage with another who will loan you their fingers to carry out great designs of music. You will loan this person your mind. The marriage will end at the first sign of sexual attraction. It will be an affectionate decoupling that will almost break the both of you. Your spouse will recover. You will not. You will die sometime between now and sixty years. Your story will matter to music.* ✿

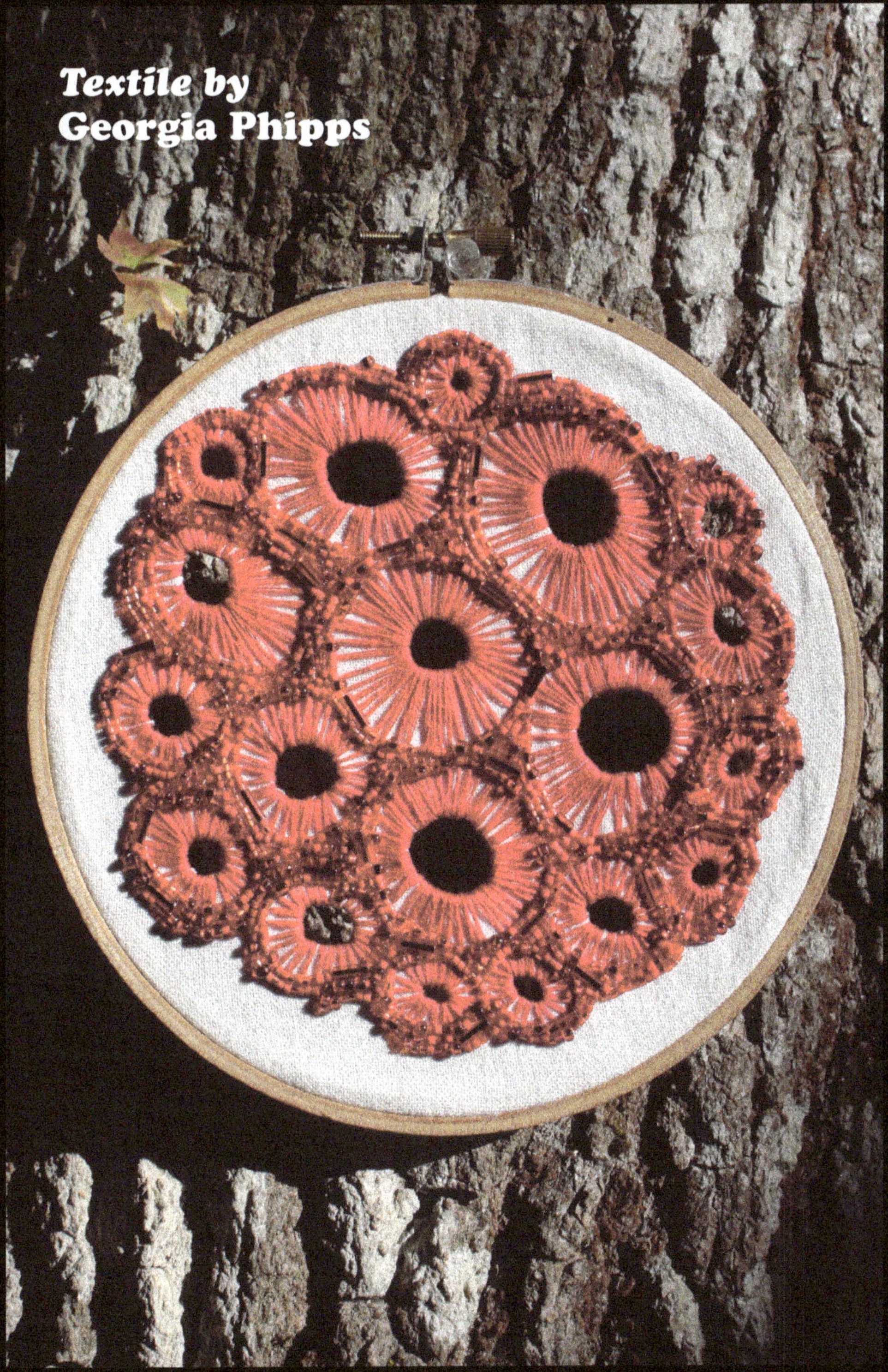

# *Textile by* Georgia Phipps

*Aggregate*
EMBROIDERY FLOSS AND DELICA SEED BEADS ON COTTON CANVAS

## Creative Non-fiction by Milo R. Muise

# The Puzzle

For the past few months, I've been assembling a puzzle on an unsteady foldout table in my apartment's entryway while a pandemic rages outside. The box's cover bears what will become the final image: an intricate web of crisscrossing lines. Upon first glance, one might describe it as a scribble, but that doesn't capture the picture's dense precision. Every mark is true black, ruler-straight. Despite it being a still image, the lines have a sense of movement, as if they are traveling, darting across each other on their singular paths. Some sections are thick with this activity, the lines forming what resembles synaptic networks, while others are stiller. In a bold red font, the box announces its name and size: "The Lines, 1000 Pieces."

Puzzlers exist at a paradoxical intersection, both a creator and an underling carrying out another's vision. You complete the puzzle, but you are not the author, and neither are you the image's artist. As with constructing a piece of furniture from IKEA, you are responsible for *assembly*, the period between the puzzle's existence in pieces and its existence as a unified whole. So, while it would be true to say upon completion that you put a puzzle together, it would be incorrect to say that you *made* the puzzle, that the finished product was entirely your doing.

Though, it would also be wrong to claim that assembly, in and of itself, is not a creative act. A puzzler is not a machine, even if a machine would likely be well-suited to puzzling. The puzzler asks, *how do I*

## *Painting by Jenene Nagy*

*approach this? From what angle? Which logic? How do I organize what seems random, meaningless, or impossibly tangled?*

I begin by finding the edge pieces, a common first step. It gives me a boundary to work within: a frame, a stage for the drama to play out.

I know this is the easiest task the puzzle will ask of me, but even so, I'm satisfied when I press the last edge piece into place. *The perimeter is secure.* I study the enclosure, its fragmented interior piled beside me in the box.

The thickest line is protected on either side by thinner ones, guardrails lining a road. Along the way, the thick line fractures into two. The hardest pieces to place are the ones that carry this change, the line's in-process transformation making it harder to classify. The lines' distinctiveness becomes disorder, an overgrown thicket crowding the view.

Thin runs parallel to thick. The former is so slight it appears gray, a diminished presence. The trick is in the gap, the distance between. I organize a gradation: so close they almost present as one, blurred; separate but intimate; distant. These distinctions are a matter of millimeters.

I spread the puzzle across the apartment, a side effect of the various lines I am "tracking." Baking pans covered in neat rows of puzzle pieces line the living room's windowsill. There are upturned boxes by the doorway, ripped cardboard refashioned into trays. As the puzzling expands, I take a photo on my phone of a connection I am hoping to find. I move between each station, comparing the pieces to the image. Sometimes, I place a promising piece on my phone screen to test whether it fits. Occasionally, it does.

I refuse to refer to the box for imagistic support, as is my self-enforced rule for any puzzle. Apparently, this is not a common form of abstinence. I take pride in the bafflement of other puzzlers, the claim that they could never, it would be *too hard*.

> "I GROW ATTUNED TO MINUSCULE DEVIATIONS IN LINE TEXTURE, ANGLE, AND TRAJECTORY. I BECOME FAMILIAR...

For a moment, I wonder whether using the box would actually make the puzzle *more* difficult, as the image is smaller and thus less detailed, unable to offer the same level of nuance as the pieces themselves. The idea is alluring, but ultimately detracts from my favorite aspect of puzzling: the interrelation between myself and the pieces, noticing where they signal that they belong together, my attention creating a connection.

The puzzle demands an intense, microscopic form of study. I grow attuned to minuscule deviations in line texture, angle, and trajectory. I become familiar with the patterns that are unique enough to be useful and those that are sufficiently ubiquitous as to be disregarded.

Relaying my strategies to my partner Katie is humorous in its difficulty. After attempting to explain, I nearly always have to refer back to the puzzle itself, show her a piece and point at the pattern I am hunting for. Even then, it often takes me marking the line with my finger while describing it—"See how that

> ...WITH THE PATTERNS THAT ARE UNIQUE ENOUGH TO BE USEFUL AND THOSE THAT ARE SUFFICIENTLY UBIQUITOUS AS TO BE DISREGARDED."

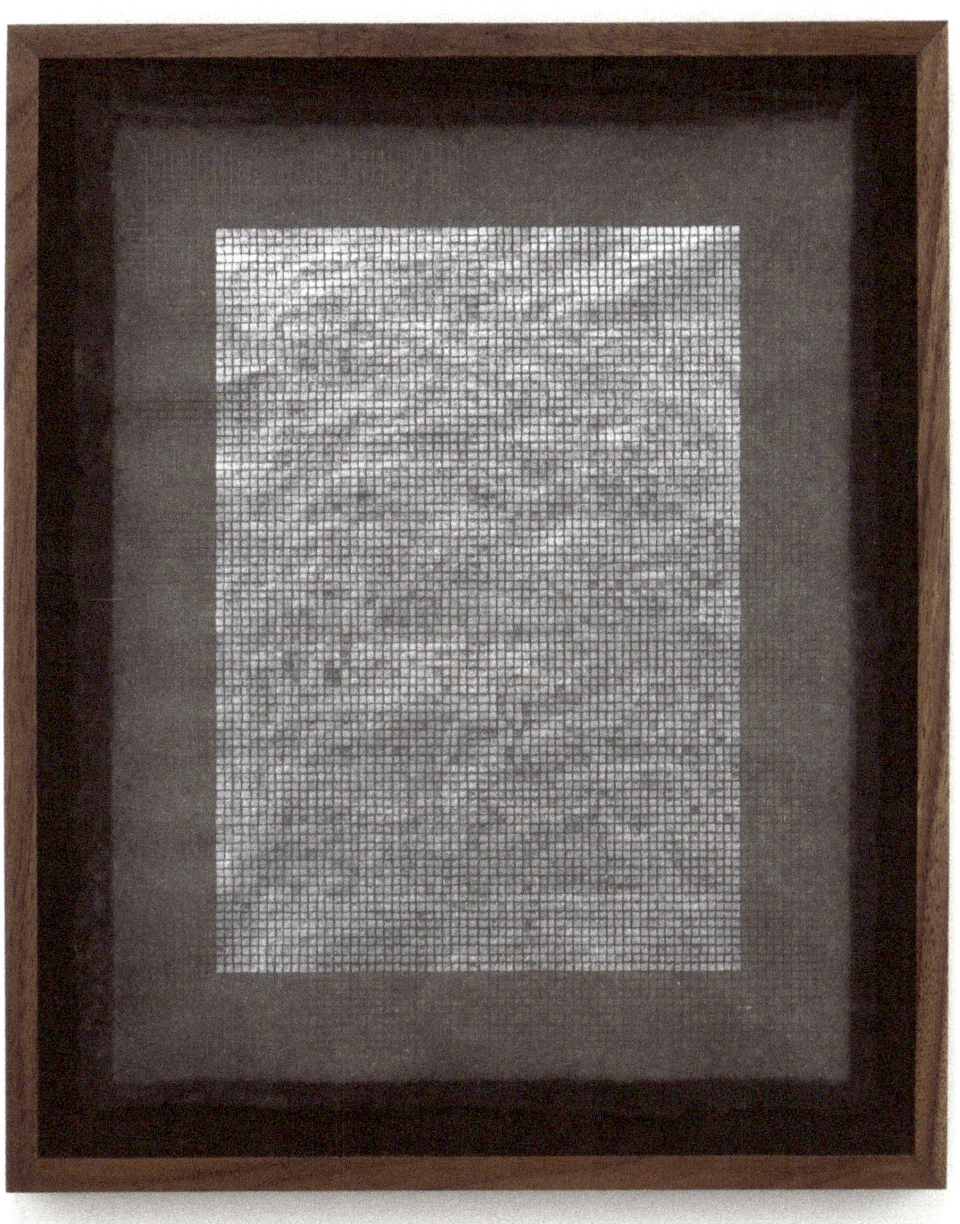

*untitled (dusk 2)*
FLASHE AND GRAPHITE ON ABACA

PHOTOS COURTESY OF
PDX CONTEMPORARY ART

one's kind of thick and that one's way thinner and they're moving diagonally, and they cut off right in the middle of this inlet?"—before she sees what I am showing her. The lines, it seems, are more precise than my language.

*Is this a waste of time?* I think every time I sort through the pieces and now, anytime I sit down to work on this essay. Friends say that anything that brings me joy isn't a waste of time, and while I appreciate the sentiment, I'm not sure I agree.

While I puzzle, *Gossip Girl* plays in the background. It is a show that operates at the nexus of pleasure and trash, fantasy and reality. The outlandish aspects of the show—its campy aesthetics, operatic emotionality, and the fact that its teen characters are constantly drinking refined cocktails publicly and without comment in swanky bars—fuse with the existence of wealth and privilege depicted. "This show really hates poor people," Katie says while we watch, and it's true—every "outsider" introduced to the core characters on the Upper East Side is eventually revealed as deceitful or conniving and is thereafter either shunned from the plot or becomes a villain. The wealthy characters' ability to hold an unbridled distaste for those below their social status *and* a limitless ability to feel victimized by this inferior class might be one of the show's most realistic facets.

Manhattan prides itself on its navigability. The streets form a logical grid, clearly named and numbered. As a tourist, I imagine I would appreciate the sense of order, but aesthetically I find it simplistic. Though I wrestle, as an adult, with Boston's many failings, I spent my childhood charmed by its frustrating impenetrability, beginning all those many years ago with the cows who decided where the roads would go, the city springing up haphazardly around their tracks. That this is likely myth rather than history doesn't diminish the fact that it seems true. The street names have little consistency, and their lettering is often close to unreadable due to weathering and lack of upkeep. Constant construction means that road closures and detours are common, rendering unfamiliar routes that might (*might*) otherwise have been straightforward. The drivers are impatient, and the people have a gruff demeanor. (Katie, born and raised in the Pacific Northwest, is constantly asking, "Are they mad at us?" whenever we interact with a server, store employee, or extended family member. I laugh every time.)

There is an honesty in giving one's more disagreeable feelings a public face. When I moved to Oregon, *I* was the one turning to Katie for reassurance whenever we came out of a conversation that *seemed* perfectly ordinary, but where I sensed an undercurrent of displeasure, some unsaid complaint that I lacked the necessary cultural education to diagnose.

**"THERE IS AN HONESTY IN GIVING ONE'S MORE DISAGREEABLE FEELINGS A PUBLIC FACE."**

Boston is a city of impossibility: there is no "right way" to do anything. Drivers yell, "Fuck you!" at pedestrians crossing the street while the walk signal is lit. To exist is to be an inconvenience is to be intolerable. On the one hand, this perspective lends itself to the quasi-suicidal belief that one's life is a burden that should be discarded for the convenience and betterment of humanity. On the other, it offers a freedom: as Kacey Musgraves once sang, "If you're damned if you do and damned if you don't, you might as well do whatever you want."

My love of puzzles began early. When I was in first grade, each member of my class made a game for the class to play. I decided to construct a jigsaw puzzle. My teacher suggested I begin by drawing the scene that my players would piece back together. She gave me examples, showed me the boxes displaying their final tableaus. I could use their pieces as a stencil over my drawing to give my pieces the classic jigsaw shape.

I had a different idea. I started with a red marker and progressed through the rainbow, scribbling layer upon layer of color across the white page until they bled together into a discordant brown. There was no pattern, no logic. Taking a hint from the snowflakes we had made in the winter, I folded the piece of paper again and again into a small square, and then I took my scissors and bisected it, then bisected those halves, then those fourths. When it was time, I swept my slivers and shards into a plastic bag and placed them on the table with my classmates' offerings.

A friend did her best to push some of the pieces around, but my puzzle was quickly abandoned in favor of my peers' neat and colorful creations. At the end of the day, I smiled at my work, its disconnected shapes, their mysterious relation to each other. It was so inscrutable even I, its creator, couldn't solve it.

"This says something about you," a friend said when I showed

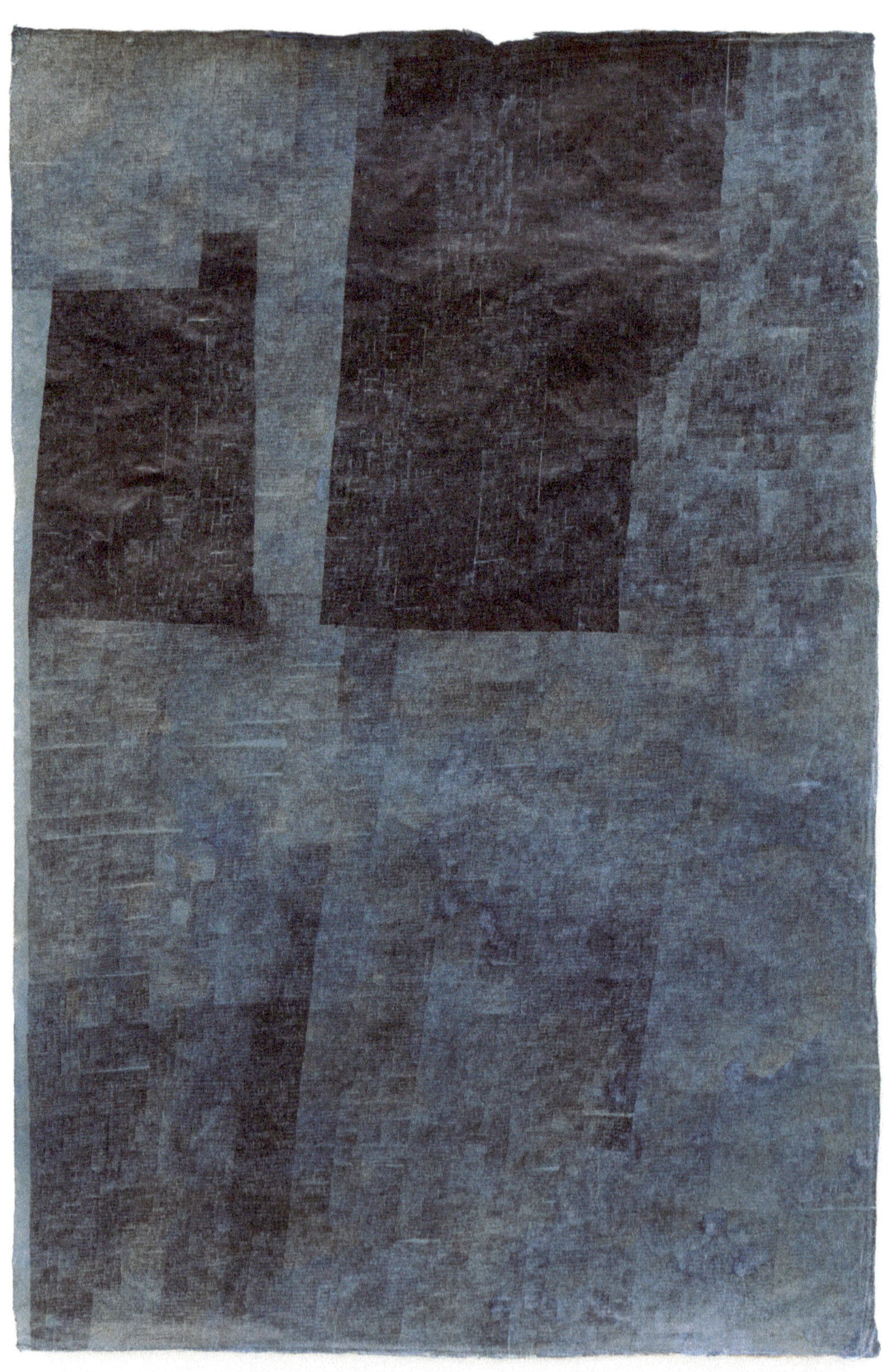

 *As our breath drifts on the wind, 4*
GOUACHE AND GRAPHITE ON ABACA

her my recent progress on The Lines. "I don't know what, but it says something."

A puzzle is not a unique entity: in most cases, it is a replica, a mass production. The same puzzle is solved over and over but in a different way each time.

Sol LeWitt took up a version of this concept in his *Wall Drawings* series. LeWitt believed an artist's idea could be its own work of art. Instead of drawing, he took his *ideas* for drawings and made them into a series of instructions. He sent these instructions to museums whose staff executed a drawing based on LeWitt's idea. As he put it, "Like an architect who creates a blueprint for a building and then turns the project over to a construction crew, an artist should be able to conceive of a work and then either delegate its actual production to others or perhaps even never make it at all."

While LeWitt's instructions were precise, they still allowed room for interpretation, meaning that the same idea would not necessarily result in identical creations.

"Wall Drawing Boston Museum" comes close to creating a version of "The Lines." These lines were dictated, but the executor (in this case, Eric Doeringer) was the one to draw each one into existence.

LeWitt might say that a puzzler is an artist, the artistry lying partially in the choices one makes in its assembly. As I put together the puzzle, I am putting together an idea.

The obvious pleasure of a puzzle is in implementing order, each piece in its place.

Is it so simple? Do I puzzle for control, for omnipotence, for the assurance that what I am after is solvable and that I have everything I need to find the solution?

Are puzzles the sitcoms of games—tidy, with problems as repeatable as they are resolvable?

In *Seinfeld*'s fourth season, Jerry and George pitch a television show that bears a meta resemblance to *Seinfeld* itself. "It's a show about nothing," George says to the network executives, self-satisfied and smiling.

When I Google this premise to check my accuracy, the results circle around a debate: Is *Seinfeld* really a show about nothing? It's a very *Seinfeld* argument to have: inane yet aware of its inanity, seething with existentialism—what constitutes "nothing"?

I joke that I am assembling a puzzle about nothing. Most puzzles have an aesthetic purpose: you complete the puzzle ostensibly because you want to complete its image, whether it be a landscape, an animal, an assortment of vegetables, a reproduction of canonical art, a beach scene populated with famous faces, or a map of the world. A puzzle's basic arc is one from nonsense (fragments) to sense (a recognizable image), and the aesthetic pleasure of the final image is part of this lucidity.

"The Lines'" visual austerity lays bare the puzzle's true purpose: difficulty for difficulty's sake.

In middle school art class, we learned about shading. Each of the room's tables had a tool placed at the center, a group of students huddled around on metal stools. From our individual vantage points, we were tasked with replicating the tool on paper, paying special attention to the shade and shadow of our instrument, the places the light didn't reach. We were to represent these darknesses four times, each time using a different shading technique: hatching, cross-hatching, stippling, smoothing.

My table had a hammer. Clawed head, dull face, handle so worn it was splintering. Midday light from the tall windows stretched in and skimmed over its body like a blanket that reveals rather than covers. Only the base of the handle, the underside of the metal claws and a thin line down the back, were untouched. A shadow spilled out and drew an off-kilter representation onto the table, otherwise bright and clean.

In our notebooks, we darkened our tools with small dots, crisscrossing and parallel lines. We pressed the edge of our pencil tips against the paper and dragged the shadows into existence. Slowly, our illustrations gained dimension, rising off the page into a semblance of reality.

I leaned over and pressed the side of my face against the table, trying a new perspective. The hammer rested on its own cheek, intimate. I looked through the long triangle created by the angle of the handle lifting off the table, a sliver of window framed by its body.

When I found the finished drawings in a stack of old schoolwork more than a decade after their creation, the stark, purposeful lines felt familiar in a way that I couldn't immediately place. My firm hand, making line after line after line.

**"I leaned over and**
**of my face against**
**new perspective.**
**rested on its own**

You can cheat at "The Lines" if you want. The back of each piece is printed with a letter, A-F, that allows you to group the pieces into sections to determine the correct orientation. I feel insulted by their presence. In protest, I keep all the pieces face up and listen to Ariana Grande's "positions" on repeat as I try fitting a piece one way, then another.

The puzzle tests my discipline, trying to taunt me with an easy (or, easier) way out. In hunger's place is an anorexic pride, my purity of spirit extinguishing all desires that detract from the virtuosity of my ambition.

**pressed the side the table, trying a The hammer cheek, intimate."**

Austrian director Michael Haneke's film *The Piano Teacher*, based on the book of the same name by Elfriede Jelinek, is a tale of discipline and the sexual chaos that erupts from the repression such dedication requires.

Isabelle Huppert's character, Erika, teaches classical piano at a conservatory in Vienna. She is aloof yet demanding with her students, and we quickly understand her stringent need for excellence as an inheritance from her mother. Despite Erika being in her early 40s, the two women live together and, more notably, share a bed. They fight like vicious teenagers over Erika's whereabouts, spending habits, and professional success (or lack thereof, in her mother's eyes). Anything that might distract Erika from her path to prominence is excised from her life, especially relationships with men.

However, The Mother's power is not absolute; sexuality leaks out of Erika. We see these liquid evacuations when she urinates by a car while teen lovers have sex inside, or when blood runs down her thigh after she cuts her genitals at home in her bathroom. When her mother calls her for dinner, she rinses off the razor and dutifully takes her seat at the table.

Erika seeks cruelty and domination until, perhaps, she doesn't. She spends much of the film seducing one of her students, persuading him to abuse her according to her violent fantasies, which are as meticulous and precise as her piano playing.

At the end, we are watching a violation, or we are watching a masochistic impulse satiated. It is even unclear to what extent the film believes its own ambiguity.

Is my interest in this puzzle one of domination or submission? Is my aim to conquer or surrender?

Do I have to choose?

When Katie offers to help, I give her what she calls the "dopamine job." I set aside a group of pieces with a specific interrelation that I believe should fit together. She is quiet for a moment, studying, then shouts, "Found one!" A brief silence, then, "Got another!" Each time she finds a connection, she receives a burst of energy that keeps her motivated. I feel it vicariously, hunched over the pieces I've organized by the window. Her success punctuates the afternoon.

IS MY INTEREST IN THIS PUZZLE ONE OF DOMINATION OR SUBMISSION? IS MY AIM TO CONQUER OR SURRENDER? DO I HAVE TO CHOOSE?

I pick a piece and scour its edges for clues, a shape or pattern to find in its partner. While I peruse my grid of singles, I visualize the absent piece: its multi-pronged outline, the lines that fan out in a V, its empty midsection. The visualization is helpful in a practical sense—having an idea of what I am looking for makes it easier to find—but there is also a hope that imagining the piece will encourage it to appear in reality. It's a borrowed lesson from my mother who, whenever we approached the mall during a busy holiday weekend, would command, "Start visualizing a parking space!" I would shut my eyes and watch our white Toyota Camry pull into the same empty spot on loop until I heard my mom say, "Aha!" then open my eyes to see my fantasy merge with reality.

As a child, I believed that my thoughts and actions transmitted symbolic messages to God, who would then interpret these messages and determine whether anyone I loved, particularly my parents, should be killed. I was under His constant surveillance, and everything I did or felt was meaningful. If I was mad at my mother, it meant that I did not appreciate her, and if I did not appreciate her, God would think it was permissible to kill her. If I did not answer my father's phone call, it meant I was rejecting his

*As our breath drifts on the wind, 1*
GOUACHE AND GRAPHITE ON ABACA

existence, which also meant God was allowed to kill him. My waking hours were filled with rituals meant to clarify to God that, no matter what He read in my mind, I wanted my parents to stay alive.

I protected them by taking my shoes on and off ten times (each foot) upon entering and exiting the house. I protected them by laying the day's dirty clothes on my bedroom floor in the shape of my body. I protected them by listening to the *Grease* soundtrack two times through nightly (only at my father's house—at my mother's I listened to a Disney read-along tape for the movie *Flubber*). I protected them by refusing to allow differing meal components to touch one another on my dinner plate. I protected them by making sure the covers on my bed fell evenly over each side. I would tug on one end, lurch to the other to confirm symmetry, lie down, then—sure that my last movements had thrown off my efforts—sit up, once again pulling the sheets this way, then back the other. I protected them by praying nightly, heaping God with gratitude for all that He had given me and only ending with a request to *please keep my mom and dad alive. I still need them and love them very much. Thank you again. Amen.* I prayed this prayer with my hands clasped with my left thumb over my right, then again with my right thumb over my left. I repeated the prayer three, five, ten times (per thumb), in case one didn't go through and to emphasize my devotion. Often, it took me over two hours to complete my nighttime rituals and trust that I could go to sleep without waking up to the news that one of my parents had died.

I found it preferable to believe that I would be culpable for any misfortune I, or those around me, suffered rather than face the fact that much of life's pain derives from random, unforeseeable circumstances. Children are especially sensitive to this powerlessness given their forced reliance on others for their basic needs and survival. I refused my role. This transposed the vulnerability of childhood onto my parents, thereby removing it from my own experience. I was safe, even if everyone around me was perpetually in danger.

As should be readily apparent, I am a Four on the Enneagram. I believe the puzzle is also a Four, though this could be a matter of projection.

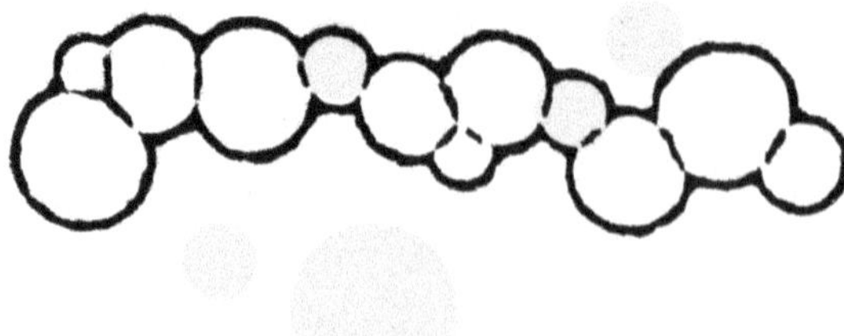

The Enneagram is a tool designed to assist in self-understanding and development. Drawing from an eclectic mix of psychological and spiritual traditions, it posits nine distinct personality types.

The pictorial depiction of the Enneagram is a circle, its perimeter labeled with the numbers one through nine. Inside, lines extend from each number, connecting each Type to two others. These lines show where a Type will integrate or disintegrate under conditions of growth or stress, respectively. For example, when Fours are under duress, we disintegrate to an unhealthy Two, typified by martyrdom and a victim complex. Alternatively, we become more principled and steadier, like Ones, when moving toward health. The Enneagram Institute website says, "The Enneagram's structure may look complicated, although it is actually simple."

Fours see ourselves as fundamentally different from others. We are both uniquely talented and uniquely flawed and derive self-value from both of these traits. No one can truly know us, no one can love us in the exact way we want to be loved, and to mask the pain of this isolation, we shape our identity around this lack, like a depressive who loathes themself while simultaneously believing they are superior to everyone around them.

I imagine "The Lines" on a shelf with other puzzles, radiating alienation. Its image is tense, alert, on guard. "I'm not like other puzzles," says "The Lines."

Fours generally steer clear of other Fours lest we discover one of our special characteristics is in fact a shared trait. Though I have several friends who are also Fours, I am quick to note that they all have a Five-Wing (Virginia Woolf, Fiona Apple), whereas I have a Three-Wing (Prince, Tennessee Williams), maintaining my distinctness even within a like-minded group. Fours with a Five-Wing, also called "The Bohemian," are reclusive, more at home in their imagination or intellect rather than "the real world." Three-Wings, or "The Aristocrat," enjoy attention and admiration while still contending with Four's withdrawn tendency, a contradiction that can result in emotional instability. A Four with a Five-Wing would complete "The Lines" in private, for self-satisfaction, whereas I post my progress on Instagram.

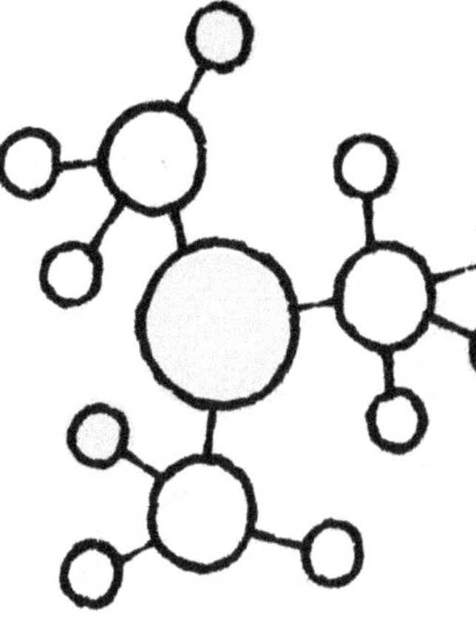

Every morning, I receive an email from The Enneagram Institute® with an EnneaThought® for my Type. The messages for Fours are frequently admonishing, harping on our self-obsessive and melancholy tendencies:

*Act today as if you experienced yourself as a stable happy person despite your many changing feelings and emotional states.*

*Emotional volatility and moodiness are not the same as real sensitivity. Keep this thought in mind today.*

*How is your Basic Desire to be yourself affecting you today? Notice if it has deteriorated into self-indulgence.*

The irony is not lost on me that I often feel victimized or misunderstood by these emails.

It is a very Four move to take on "The Lines," and it is similarly Four-ish to feel pride at receiving this text:

*Your puzzling is extremely intense*
*That puzzle terrifies me*

My strong identification with Type Four is incongruent with the Enneagram's aims. The Enneagram is not about being the best version of your type but to integrate healthy aspects of *all* the types into your personhood. This is an especially difficult task for Fours due to our anxiety around identity—our Basic Fear is that we have no identity or personal significance. Our self-proclaimed uniqueness is a defense against this fear. Integration, then, becomes synonymous with a loss of identity, which is synonymous with insignificance, which ultimately translates to death.

Many of my Type Four tendencies are reinforced by my Scorpio moon placement: intensity, deep feeling, a desire for intimacy at odds with an equally powerful desire to protect oneself against any potential harm that could arise in interpersonal relationships.

While there is no overt methodological link between astrology and the Enneagram, they are both systems of knowledge shaped by understandings outside dominant, "reasonable" logic and offer insight into one's personhood and life path. Among queers, if you're into astrology, you're probably also into the Enneagram—and if you're anti the former, you likely feel the same way about the latter.

Most casual astrology users simplify their chart to their Sun sign, though this only informs one's public-facing identity, and even then, the sign's characteristics can be mitigated or exaggerated by other factors in their astrological makeup. For example, Katie's Sun is in Gemini, but she doesn't really manifest as a Gemini because of the way her Taurus placements ground Gemini's more erratic traits—and this is still a simplification that could be further complicated, if space and scope allowed.

*Is this a waste of time?* I think as I read my horoscope at the start of each week.

In *Recaps Magazine*, academic Christopher J. Lee asks, "Is it by coincidence that astrology is widely practiced amongst queers? And is it by coincidence that those queers who practice astrology do so sarcastically, sometimes, but sometimes earnestly, sincerely, and devotedly?" On its face, astrology seems antithetical to the typical queer suspicion of prescription and rigid identity categories. For Lee, queers look to the stars not just as an escape, a "fragile but precious alternative—at once intricate and unconvincing, a kind of cheap fiction lacking the force to supplant our current world order," but also because we occupy a similar space in the social imagination. We identify with astrology because together we are suspect and trashy, *outcasts*, *tasteless*. We long for a way of naming ourselves outside of the structures that have harmed us and those we love.

There is also a campy pleasure in taking seriously what, within a modern Western context, is supposed to be for entertainment; making meaningful what others see as frivolous.

> "WE IDENTIFY WITH ASTROLOGY BECAUSE TOGETHER WE ARE SUSPECT AND TRASHY, OUTCASTS. TASTELESS."

Still, it doesn't align with my personal ideology to reduce astrology to a fiction. More accurate is to call it a narrative, a way of looking, a method of self-organization. Like most narratives, it can be read didactically or with complexity. My chart is not a flat summary of my personhood. But I *will* joke about my Mercury in Leo when I'm holding court at a party, or my Venus in Cancer when I talk about what has kept Katie and I together for so long. When I look at my chart, I feel a sense of recognition. In its lines, I see myself.

As the puzzle approaches completion, I switch perspectives, micro to macro. I stay at a distance, surveying, spotting patterns that only announce themselves over a large swath of pieces. They need to be in context to be recognized as related, dense thickets of lines suddenly given shape, an arc, a direction.

As I've puzzled, I've considered it a given that the puzzle's image is incoherent, or that the puzzle requires a discipline to complete that its image lacks. This understanding depends on how I conceptualize the image's scale. The lines might appear aimless or without a governing pattern because they are a distant representation of their content. Zoomed out, they resemble long-exposure photography of cities at night, each line a pair of headlights journeying

"I stay at a distance, surveying, spotting patterns that only announce themselves over a large swath of pieces.

They need to be in context to be recognized as related, dense thickets of lines suddenly given shape, an arc, direction."

from origin point to destination. Or they might represent a more sexual form of traffic, a la The Chart, Alice Pieszecki's record of "interconnectivity" as seen on the classic lesbian melodrama *The L Word.*

The Chart documents the sex lives of LA lesbians and those who are welcomed into their beds. Each name is connected to another via a line, signifying a sexual encounter. Many of the relationships intertwine—Carolynn is connected to both Lisa P. and Heather, who are also connected to one another, and who also have both had sex with Lauren—poking fun at the enmeshment and insularity stereotypical of lesbian communities.

In season five, Control Freak Business Top, Bette Porter, cheats on Hot Sculptress, Jodi Lerner, with her boring long-term ex, Tina "I Wish I Wasn't a Lesbian (But I Also Can't Utter the Term 'Bisexual')" Kennard. When Bette finally breaks up with Jodi, Jodi claims that it is impossible for Bette to love both her and Tina at the same time and vows that Bette is the only woman Jodi will ever (and has ever) loved. The scene singlehandedly undoes Jodi's entire characterization, which had centered around her free-spirited nature and love of the unorthodox, including non-monogamy. To have Jodi suddenly renounce her previously entrenched belief system is less an example of character development and more indicative of the show's general confusion about the desire for any relationship structure outside of the closed couple.

My critique falters at the question: *what did I expect? The L Word* is not known for its realistic portrayals of lesbian and queer life—beyond the improbable wealth of the main cast and its bizarrely white portrayal of LA, everything from breast cancer to early-transition facial hair is treated with a healthy dose of artistic license despite the theme song's lyrics staking a claim on realism: *it's the way that we live.*

Regardless, the stumbles over non-monogamy felt more pronounced during my most recent rewatch, timed as it was with a devastating romantic dissolution that echoed Jodi's about-face. It is frustrating to see the way cultural misconceptions about polyamory leech into one's belief systems about relationships, trust, and love, making it even more challenging to effectively practice non-monogamy. When difficulty arises, it is easy to feel like it is because poly is a doomed enterprise and that I'm foolish for even trying, sapping me of the stamina required to navigate and resolve conflict.

When I tell people I'm poly, the most common response echoes that of my puzzling: *I could never, it sounds so hard,* which, of course, it can be—though, so can any relationship. It is challenging to build and sustain intimacy with others, period. More than that, the work of polyamory is a

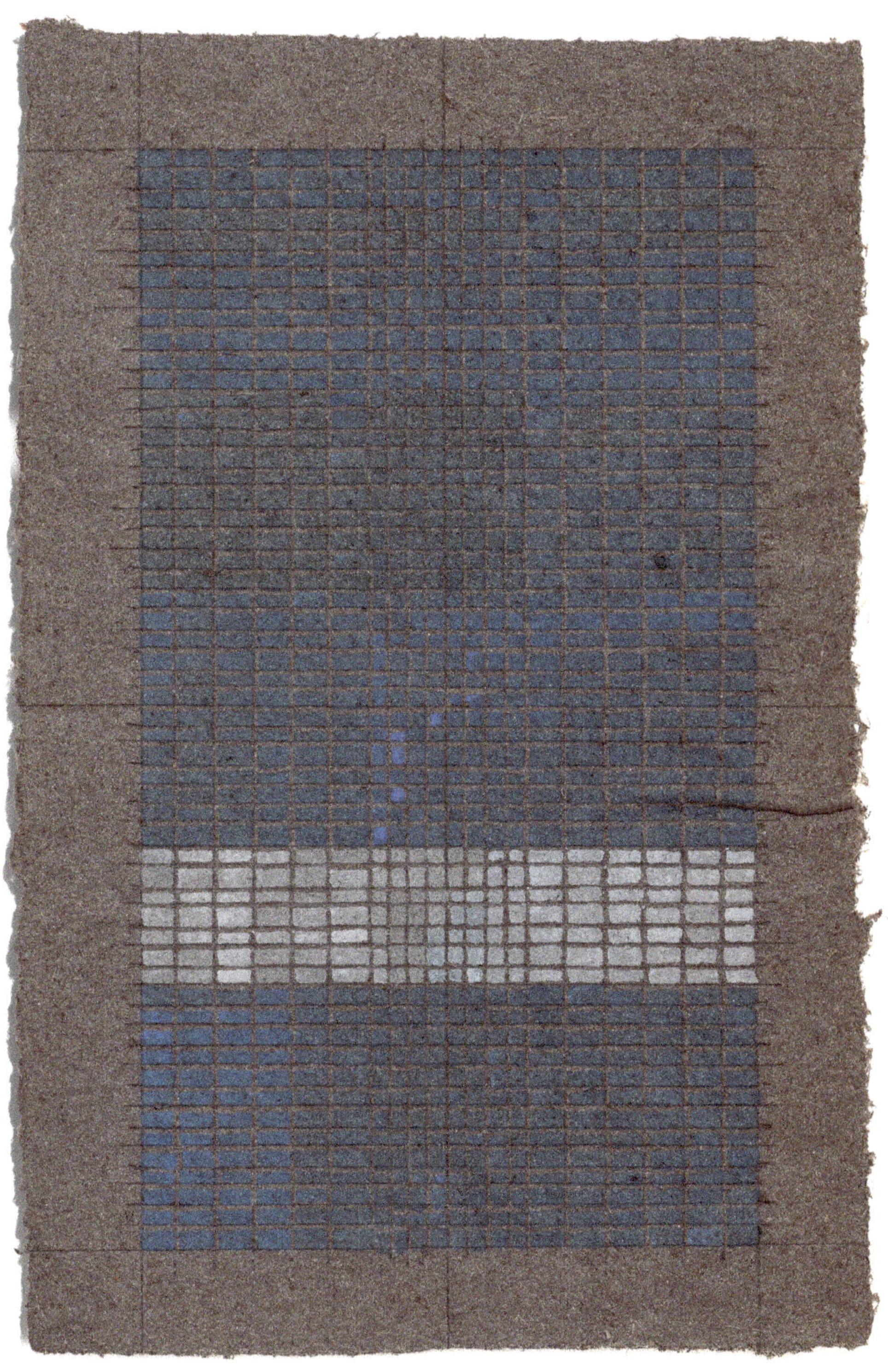

*untitled (air 2)*
GOUACHE AND GRAPHITE ON ARTIST MADE PALM FROND PAPER

> "WHEN I TELL PEOPLE I'M POLY, THE MOST COMMON RESPONSE ECHOES THAT OF MY PUZZLING: I COULD NEVER. IT SOUNDS...

> ...SO HARD, WHICH, OF COURSE, IT CAN BE—THOUGH, SO CAN ANY RELATIONSHIP."

labor that, while sometimes exhausting and demanding, I find rewarding. It is productive: rather than spending my energy defending against the fears that undergird most relationships (what if my partner falls in love with someone else? How do I know my partner really loves me? Are they trustworthy?), in polyamory I can move through those fears, changing my relationship to them and their potency. I build trust not through keeping my partner contained within a strict set of parameters and rules, but through acknowledging her freedom to explore and her freedom to return to me.

I finish the puzzle on March 21, 2021. I know this date because I posted a video to Twitter: I hold up the piece to the camera, a thicket of black against white, then pan down to the table, the puzzle covering its surface save for one small gap in the middle where the blue tablecloth peeks through. I tap the piece into place triumphantly then step back, taking in my accomplishment.

In truth, the video documents the second time I placed the final piece. The first, Katie held my phone as I preambled about the puzzle, restarting multiple times to change the angle, or the lighting, or to sound less rehearsed. My irritation was visible by the time we shot the climactic moment. She paused the recording, and I dug the piece out with my nail, returning the puzzle to its incomplete status.

"Just let me do it myself," I said.

I buy puzzle tape, large sticky sheets to hold the puzzle in place. My plan is to frame and then hang it in my living room, a testament to my five months of dedication. Because the sheets affix to the back of the puzzle, the puzzler must find a way to turn the puzzle facedown. The internet suggests sandwiching the puzzle between two large sheets of cardboard and then flipping it upside down, but I don't have cardboard large enough. Seeing no other option, I detach a chunk of pieces from one of the corners and set them on the floor, backside-up. I take another cluster and move it to the floor, connecting it to the first. A few loose pieces fall to the floor, and I finally allow myself to use the "cheat" letters printed on the backs to help determine where they fit. I move from the table to the floor for hours, slowly reassembling the puzzle a few feet to the right.

Later, I tell a friend about the ordeal. In the middle of my story, she interrupts, asking, "Why didn't you call me? I could have come over and helped!"

The puzzle sits under my bed, waiting for its frame.

By opting to freeze "The Lines" in a state of completion, I am sacrificing an aspect of puzzling I find especially delightful: the fact that one spends all this time putting an image together only to, upon its articulation, disassemble it. The pieces go back into the box and become a jumbled mess that, if the desire struck, could be taken out and assembled again.

The puzzle's integrity is ephemeral, and its ephemerality paradoxically heightens and diminishes its import. I think it's an error to argue, as I may have earlier, that the coherent image is "the point" of puzzling. So much of puzzling is invested in the process, the *doing* rather than the *done*.

To puzzle is to perplex, to confound, to dwell in the space between hypothesis and certainty. I look again at the image on the box, its baffling network of lines. I find "The Lines" most bewildering when it is finished. ✿

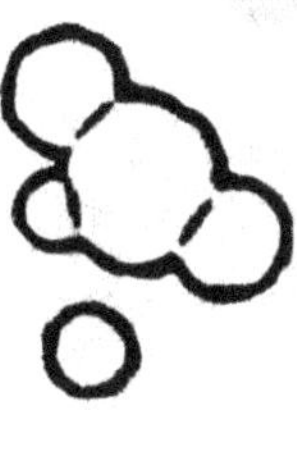

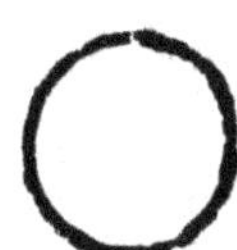

**Fiction by**
**Thea Prieto**

# Teeth

Three months of sour refusals, four nights of cold seething, and somehow Sayer has arrived early to her first group counseling session. A windowless waiting room lined with tailbone chairs, a metal table stacked with talk-driving caffeine and larynx-lubing juices—Tell me how you really feel, my small square napkin, my minuscule sugar packet? Fuck me, are we really going to wave out our loved ones like wringed hankies, make their dead bodies trot to the tune of our fondest maybe-days, these memory-papered dolls, sad marionettes dancing with hollow, wooden clogs. *Clunky, clunky*, please come back to me. Just go inside to get Mom off your back. Sit in a circle and tell strangers that your secret keeper was hit by a drunk driver. Pull up all the pink days and the Someday plans and turn what's left of your husband into a yellowed file, a crumpled sign-in sheet, recycled holidays blackened with useless, desperate groping. You can't grip water to make it hold still.

Talk about it. Fine. She'll open her mouth, *Fine*, talk for her two kids, *Fine*, talk for her mother. Touch the surface in front of these strangers, because guess what: ripple days today, ripple days tomorrow.

8:51 AM. Sayer sharpens herself into a chair facing the conference room door marked GRIEF SUPPORT, the only free resource in her area that month, and kneads her blistered palms out of fists. Sixty-nine minutes. Her truck will sit in front of this rural community center for sixty-nine minutes, only have to do this for sixty-nine minutes. Sixty-eight minutes. A mutilated paperclip to monkey the long redwood splinter in her thumb meat, an angry sliver too large to overlook, too deep to subtract. Her first day back on the job site, her mind on car accidents instead of sawing blades and biting lumber (footsteps in the waiting

***Painting by***
**Rachel Warkentin**

room—*Nevermind*), and now the skin is pale, ringed an inflamed and anxious red. Infected. It's too late now, do you see what you've done? It's pus-rot infected. Leave it alone, making it worse—*Who cares*, anything but the woman pacing, existing, noisy with being. Ignore the splinter, don't want to know where it came from, don't want to know why others want counseling, her footsteps squeaking the tight waiting room carpet. A middle-aged woman with cropped greasy hair, her cheeks already wet, white lips mouthing ghost hopes (God, please don't let us recognize each other). Look away, think of work, work at your splinter, look at it, don't want to—*Just hold this water still.*

Everything is fine. She's fine. The splinter will be fine.

Another half cup of coffee, drenching a chemical tongue and sour-threaded throat. Sayer shivers a few breaths and returns to her corner seat, to wait for them, whoever they'll be. They're going to tell you Anger and Denial, like you're some kind of idiot. They're going to tell you Anxiety and Depression and Natural To Feel This Way, like you're a child, like you're acting like a child, like you can't stop bawling like a child. There's a girl here now, flapped into the waiting room with rubber sandals blister-snapping. Can't be more than sixteen years old. Can't believe this, can't believe I'm missing work for this, to sit here with crying children, had enough of the crying, my mom and kids already crying when the hospital called, I can't believe I threw the phone at my mom—

Stop. Stop rippling. Flex ear canals to fog and dull sound. Get through, be through, don't be a child, just a child. Sixteen years, can't have lost what you lost, has no idea, no idea what you've lost, what you've lost, you've lost—

Sayer's fingers zap away from

# "A mutilated paperclip to monkey the long redwood splinter in her thumb meat...

her splinter and secretly number off nightmares into the air, the list of horrors she will give up if they really want them, enough to fry them sober. ONE: his body creased inside the flipped vehicle when it lights on fire, TWO: still alive when the paramedics pull him from the wreck fifteen minutes later, THREE: I'm late to the hospital, he's alone when—STOP, please, stop. Don't want to know these things, these burning billboard terrors, this sobbing woman, this sixteen-year-old child—your mother told you to come here, didn't she? Your mother told you to talk to someone, talk to anyone, because your kids are crying, they miss their father, they're too young to understand, is Dad going to be alright?

She ignites to her feet so quickly the sixteen-year-old across the room flinches. Scared eyes meet briefly, then bounce away—birds dipping off powerlines. Sayer realizes how full her lungs are. Three painful breaths: Fine, Fine, Fine. Calm down. Throw your coffee cup away. Three steps to the garbage can, noises joining together in the waiting room. The middle-aged woman is still pacing the floor, squeaking. The sixteen-year-old is looking at her cell phone, shuddering. They are both hurting, God, don't look—hurting and you don't know, you don't know, I'm so—crumpled napkin—so, so angry. Can't sleep at night.

Back in her chair, Sayer's jittering work boot pumps a pocket in the thin carpet, air releasing through the tight-wound fabric like a rapid pulse. 8:56 AM. Soon now. Will need to talk soon (Don't speak) to tamp it down or spew vats of gut-melting anger. Just sixty-four minutes to find out. Chin up, shoulders back, dance to this goddamn tune. There's an elderly man sitting in the waiting room, crept in around the perimeter (Don't trust them) baldness and drooped eyes, white hair curled at his temples, like my grandfather.

Grandpa would never have agreed to this, would have taken it out on his work, taken care of his family, stayed silent—

Silent, like the pain in his stomach (*Don't think about that now*) the cancer he tried to keep a secret. Internal organs bloated, septic, didn't want his family to see him like that

**...an angry sliver too large to overlook, too deep to subtract."**

(*Think of something else*) didn't want to talk—Grandpa's favorite granddaughter.

Stop thinking. Talking wouldn't have helped him anyway *Don't be a child* didn't want me there *Wasn't there* can't help him now, can't think about this, crashing *You weren't there to help him.*

No, please, not this—nothing to do with it, he didn't want anyone's help *Should have been there* he was by himself, driving alone and running town errands for our family *Should have been our accident.* Wish we had stayed home more often, hadn't worked so much, always wishing for more time with the kids, no rushing and driving, just long arms and warm sheets and fingers lacing and whispering, whispering and now never, never—

Crashing. Searing. Can't grip water to make it hold still.

9 AM. When Sayer smears the wet from her burning face, she sees the others have already disappeared through the wagging door to the conference room. *Alone*, she thinks, as her guilt crawls the empty waiting room, pressing flush against her cold and lonely skin. This pitiful, painful fuel—there isn't even much of it. Her watery vision shrinks and softens the door even as Sayer finally approaches it, each hesitant step contracting it smaller—now it is a child's door, now a jammed car window, now a closed mouth. She reaches for the round doorknob, which is studded with jagged white spikes, the barbs chalky like sea coral except the pitted bone is human. She wraps her splintered palm around the clustered incisors, the sharp canines and grooved molar teeth, and tightens her sore fingers around the prickled device. The knob turns, the latch pops, and the space beyond opens its voice. ✿

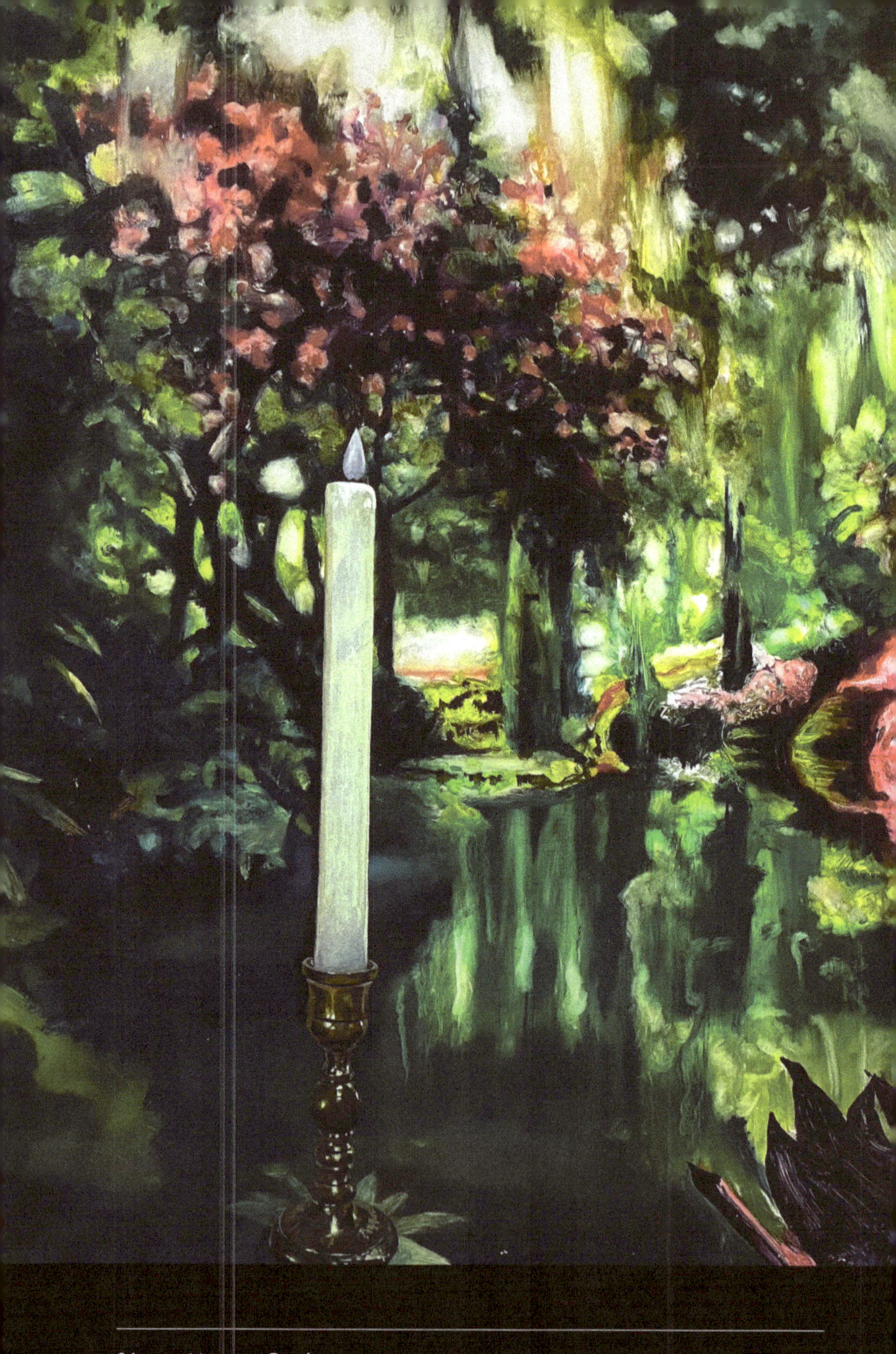

 *Memory Garden*
OIL PAINT ON PANEL

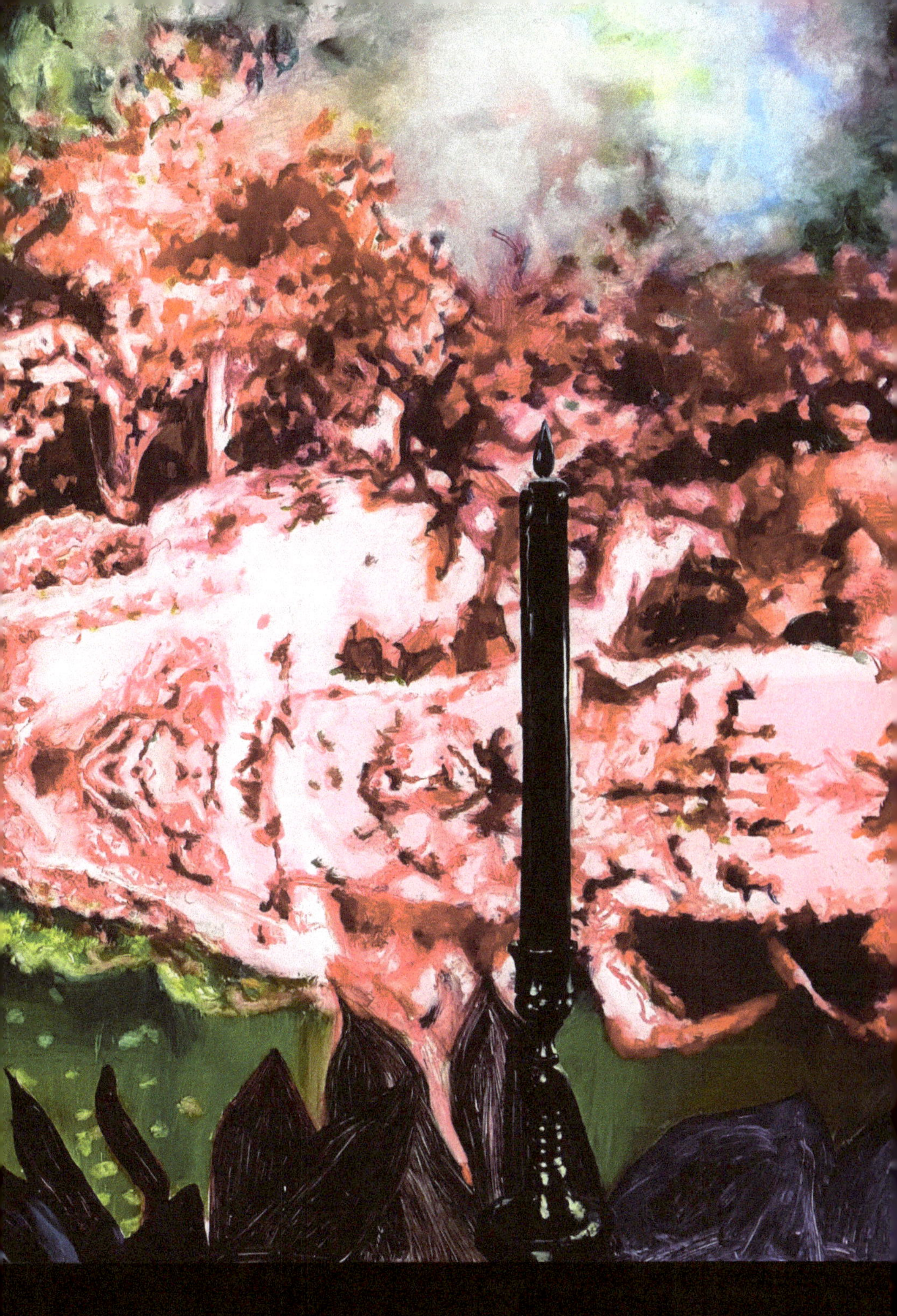

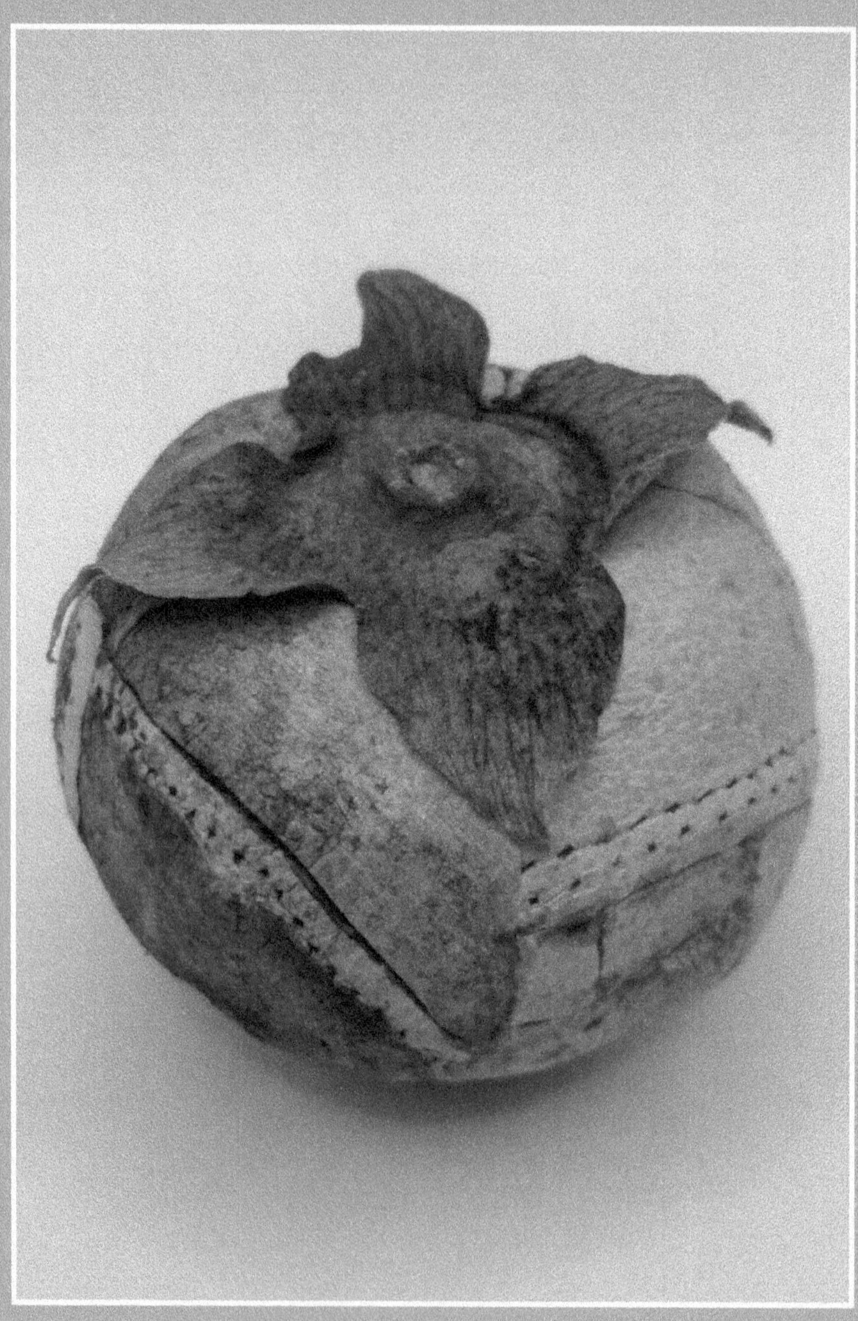

## Sculpture by Maxwell Kline



*Persimmon Two*
RECYCLED LEATHER FROM CAT-SKIN GLOVES, POLYMER CLAY, ALUMINUM FOIL, SALT-CURED PERSIMMON CALYXES, BEESWAX, MOD PODGE, AND MATTE GEL MEDIUM

### *Absently, the Light*

comes from wherever you gathered me, here
finding a path of living.

always stuck before importance,
I wish I could provide a technical story to children at night.
    I'm speaking of threads graded against skin, the
    lame room, a worsening flu.

winding time around witness,
discover a live whale beached, a mass collapsing itself. with
    strong curiosity, people gathered round, considering
    their lamps
    displacing sadness by the light.

the others crowded waterside herding
around a missing speaker, absent
memory fat

**Poetry by**
**Emma Riskin**

## *Stomach Letter*

Teeth behind tongue

A complicated way to say
(you were speaking).

When dreaming in the early hours
A pillow tells
        (the tongue inside the teeth)
About the pink taste
        The manner of curiosity: not quite red.

In the stomach,
I could taste.

Cow licks calf
fur wet with a line
Like this–
        Wet grain on tongue,
        Unrelated to soup-
        (Soup): warm liquid around the tongue.
        Cheeks puffed: this is tongue soup.
        Distinct from "tongue soup"
        (Tongue soup): moving the severed (cow) tongue upon the stable tongue,
        grains against grains to stomach.

Unlike you,
who moved your tongue pink against mine
even behind my teeth            (as a mouth might look shut)

Red pungency in the mouth, stomach burbling

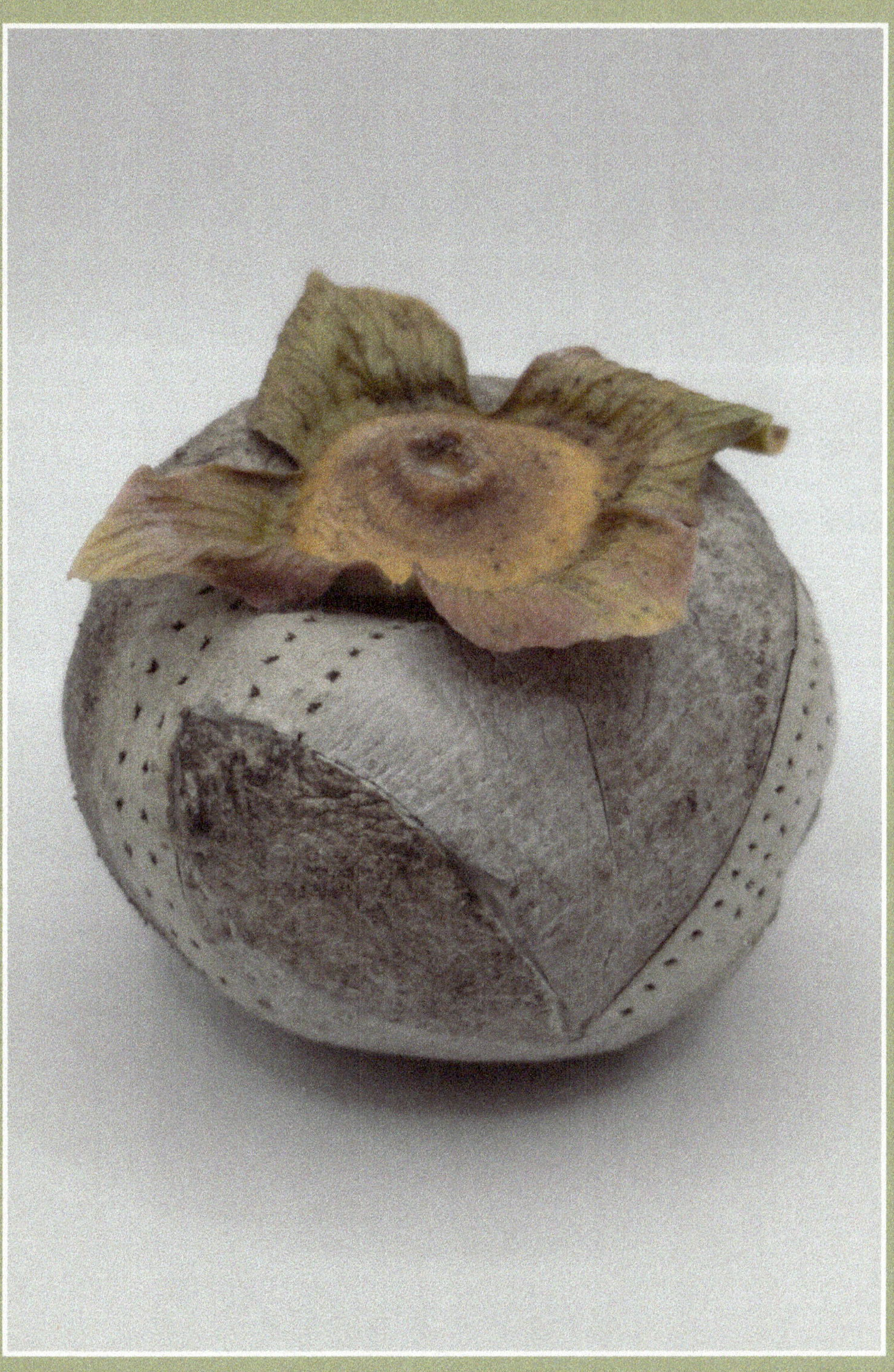

*Persimmon Three*
RECYCLED LEATHER FROM CAT-SKIN GLOVES, POLYMER CLAY, ALUMINUM FOIL, SALT-CURED PERSIMMON CALYXES, BEESWAX, MOD PODGE, AND MATTE GEL MEDIUM

**Fiction by**
**Noah Jordan**

# Our Summer

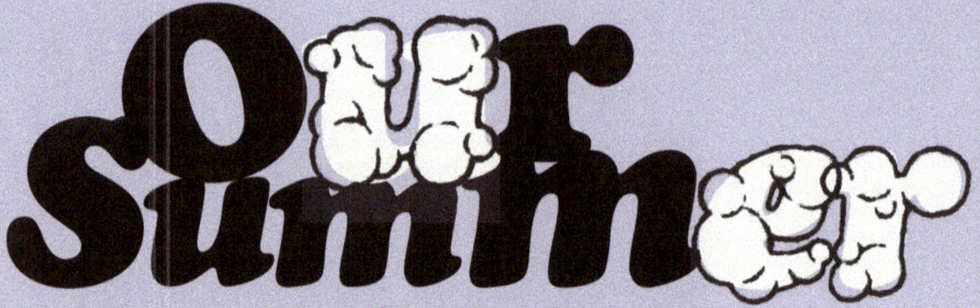

Some of us got an allowance. Some of us were virgins. Some had cystic acne. Some had taken the SAT. We walked around with our Adam's apples out, wartime expressions. Classes were out and there was nothing to do except for what we wanted. It was going to be our summer and it started on the football field behind the school. The sun was down but there was enough streetlight to recognize each other.

J got our attention by saying the gas station up the road stacked racks of beer right next to the emergency exit. He was a year younger than us and had a small drooping mouth, few friends. When he ran out with a rack in each fist we whooped and sprinted into the neighborhood, J in the back with 48 Rolling Rocks.

He let us in the side door when the light in his parents' window went out. The stairs down were done in a slick gray paint and each made a different creak. The basement room was long and narrow with wood panel walls and a char-marked shag carpet. J's older brother Ro passed out half-bars of Xanax, said he didn't necessarily feel great about doing it. Some of us struggled to swallow them. There was no clean water in the basement. We sat and watched each other, waited. Then morning sunlight angled down through the dirty egress windows, and we struggled awake with the sense that something revolutionary had happened. It startled a few kids that we didn't see again. The rest of us understood that this was growing up and were back the next night, fast friends.

## Printmaking by Taylor Wallau

The first time J's dad came down to yell he didn't kick us out, and we knew he wasn't a real threat. We only pretended to be scared when he came down again the next night. We secreted the pills when we heard him coming. Mostly he was mad about the noise, secondarily about all the smoke. After a week he stopped coming down. J's mom never bothered. Sometimes we'd see her feet through the egress windows in the mornings, heels dragging a wheeled briefcase behind, slow.

We were in that basement most of June. There were a lot of us and J said who could come. He became capricious. Every day a slightly different group of us was allowed down. J'd say cruel things to one of us and then look at the rest of us to laugh, which we did. He didn't listen to a word anyone said except for Ro. It was the time of his life, surrounded by new friends.

In July we got programmatic. We assembled a stable memory of what we liked about being high, the silky bodily hum, the deep quiet in our heads, and learned to sustain it deep into nights, to get it back in the morning with more weed and nicotine. We got our hands on styrofoam cups and something that was supposed to be lean. We played music. We focused on listening, coin-slot eyes. We realized our favorite songs had been talking about these pills, these liquids, that there was an entirely new segment of Soundcloud we could relate to, that the peace we were finding was part of what we admired in our favorite artists. Our nights fuzzed out same as theirs.

Things like milligrams started to matter around the time Ro got kicked out of the house. It was a fight that did it. We pulled bongs and other breakables beyond the arc of J's swinging arms and watched his punches bound off Ro, never quite hitting square. The big brother waited, then threw two jabs that sat J down on the coffee table, a hook that laid him sideways on the shag. Then he started kicking. Once J's dad had Ro pinned to the ground he asked us what the hell we were good for, if not to break up a fight. Ro had been drinking rum all night. His expression was goofy and smiling, and he was still trying to hook an arm back up around his dad's red, veined head. We were out of there fast. J came running after us, bleeding bad, asking if we could take him somewhere. There wasn't another house for us to go to but there was a park on the bluffs above the trainyard and the river. We sat and smoked while he calmed down and the bleeding stopped. Then we took him back.

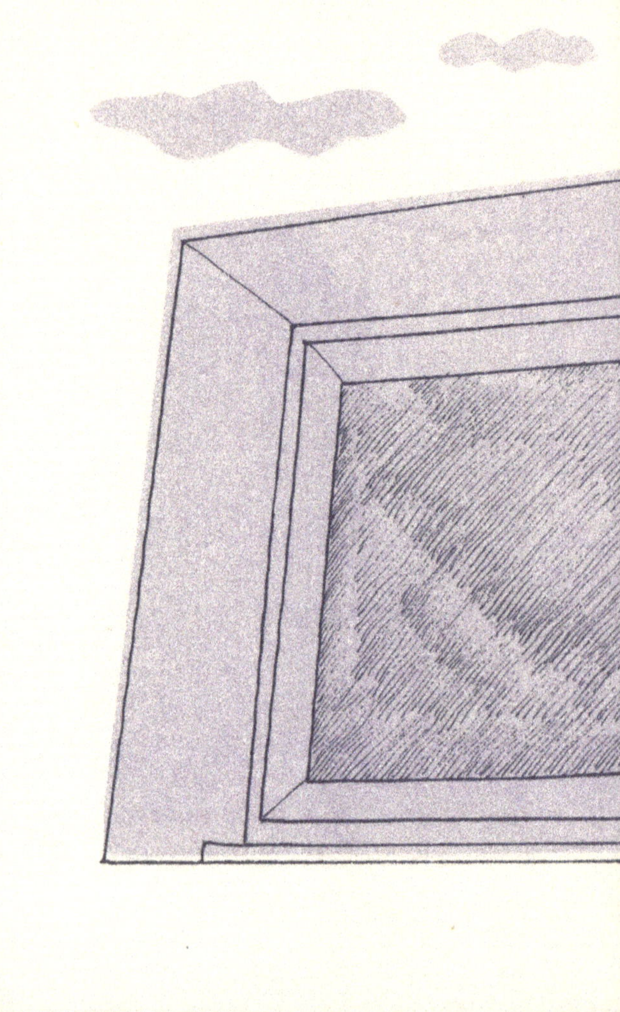

We found sources to replace Ro easily: a kid from a rival school with a small head and metal pill box, a middle-aged man who hung up if we forgot his code-words, upperclassmen with girlfriends who ferried things out of car windows. One dealer approached us at the park, ambiguously aged with dirty fingernails he used to pluck his pills out of the gallon bag he kept them in. He rattled on about effects and production processes until we stopped him, explained that we just wanted Percocet. He blinked, and then pinched a round bluish pill from the bag and said that it was basically Percocet. It wasn't at all, but it was tremendous. We took his next few recommendations and started to see the bigger picture. We tried different colors and sizes, roots and prefixes and brand names. Our tastes refined. We stopped sharing with each other. Cash got tight.



*Night Window*
TWO-COLOR RISOGRAPH PRINT

**"He blinked, and then pinched a round bluish pill from the bag and said that it was basically Percocet. It wasn't at all, but it was tremendous."**

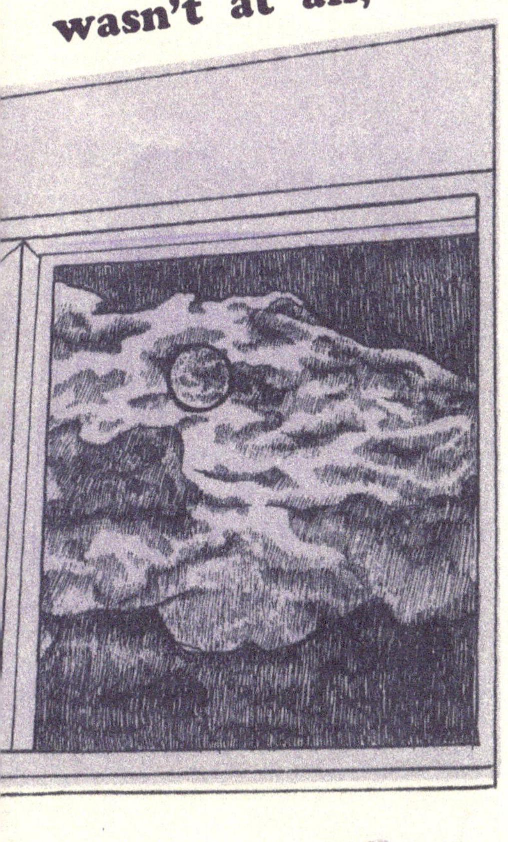

Something like boredom crept in, but it wasn't the boredom we knew. We were unsure how to resolve it until one night on a walk back to J's from a deal in the park one of us pulled on a car handle and it opened. We found brandless sunglasses and three phone chargers. Later we found 24-hour markets with slow clerks, a head shop with a pryable back door. We broke windows and flew out of emergency exits. We pushed rising freshmen down onto hard summer grass and they always gave up their cash easily.

One night a kid with grimy shoes we teased him about, a kid who'd been with us all summer, brought out the money his parents had pulled together for his 17th birthday. He showed it to us, actually held it up. The kid was called Hog for his resemblance. It was the most money he'd had at once and he didn't know how to handle himself. He always fell asleep first. The wallet would hardly shut it was so full, but it slid from his pocket easily. He searched frantically the next morning and understood only when he sat panting against the wall and noticed us watching him. He stood unsteadily, took his ratty backpack and climbed up out of J's basement into the bright early morning, off to sneak back in his window before his parents checked. We never spoke about it and Hog never asked.

**"Classes started. The clouds came back. The spark went into the first leaves...**

It was smoky all August. None of us had seen smoke like that in our city, then. J's parents took a camping trip to get out from under it and Ro reappeared. He was calm and happy that night and we realized we'd missed him. He had the good sense, as he felt himself fading, to lock his old bedroom door. He had the bad sense to assume that none of us had learned to pick locks. The door's lock, a cam lock in an old home, was trivial. We spread his weed out and removed the least conspicuous buds, spread his pills out and took from the varieties he seemed to have a lot of. J stood in the bedroom doorway as we did this. When we were done he knelt and returned what was left to their bags, rolled and stowed them the way he knew Ro did.

That same weekend J's mom's jewelry collection got picked through. The police pulled footage from the pawn shop where it turned up and brought her a still of the clerk spreading her emerald collar wide on the glass case. She fixed the still to the fridge using a photo magnet of her wearing the same collar at a wedding. In it, on the other side of the case, stood a squat, grainy form that was clearly J. J's mom failed to identify him. She got more serious about keeping us out.

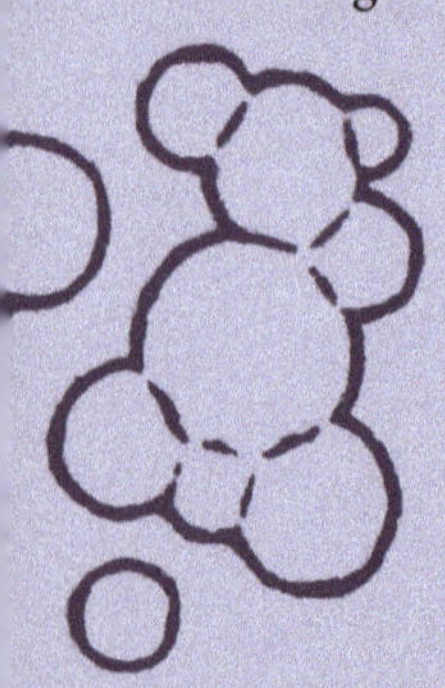

We sat in parks or on street corners. We drove around the city and up into the hills. Our parents didn't like it. There was a new edge in town, they said. The paper was calling it a summer of lawlessness. New tents, lines of them now, overnight arrivals. It didn't scare us. We thought it was exciting in a disgusting way.

Some nights J could have a few of us over. We had to show up early and come through the front door. His parents were always friendly when we passed them on the way down. We discovered his basement was an impossible place to be when it wasn't full.

The night that a kid none of us knew from a different school on the other side of town died, we sat on the bluffs above the trainyard and the river. More of us were supposed to come but they didn't. J hadn't been specifically invited but was there. Someone played music on a small speaker and pale bands of sky moved on the water. When the darker blues started to drag west people stood up and left. J stayed the longest, watched the trains pull through the navy yard.

The kid's name was Walker. The memorandums we saw online said he liked board games and the outdoors. They didn't say how he died, but we heard he had a summer like ours. Parents started to put the pieces together. People said crisis was on the move. Obama proposed a billion in new funding to address prescription opioid abuse. Some of us started looking into college applications or fall sports or girlfriends. Several were sent to outpatient camps. Some splintered off and kept going. Whatever direction, they went silently. It happened fast. Classes started. The clouds came back. The spark went into the first leaves and those that watched understood for the first time what it means for summer to become fall.

**...and those that watched understood for the first time what it means for summer to become fall."**

In October three kids sat in J's car under the streetlight white and passed the bong from seat to seat. J released the smoke and it sunk in an arc. He shut his eyes and let his head hang. The smoke piled on the dash and swept upward at the edges.

"Should we see what the other boys are doing?" J asked with his eyes shut. Nobody responded. One kid produced the dime bag J had given him and dug with his index finger for the round blue pill. The other two bumped hands reaching for the bong in J's lap. The street was wet and there were leaves in the gutter. A dog walker knocked on the driver's side window and told them to get going. J started the car and rolled it slowly from the curb, turned the corner and looked for the next place to park. ✿

## *After Sunan al-Tirmidhī 1668*

Children whisper
into voids of rubble
they carry the hope
that the pinch of
an insect bite could
really be a bomb's feel
their mothers name
martyrs now.

**Poetry by**
**Josh Cox**

### *No Angel Song I*

I see angels    and                I say get the rope
There's trees without adornment
There's leaves without                last breath
Swaying bodies        make the breeze better
It's a beautiful day    when I see blood                tinged feathers in the wind It's a
beautiful day            when I hear kids        clamor and        see faces filled with smiles
we picnic and we party and we dance It's
better than any carnival or county fair
this God given fun is such a blessing
I promise        the lord *loves* a lynching- just
like            me.

**_Drawing by_**
**Bell Mayrer**

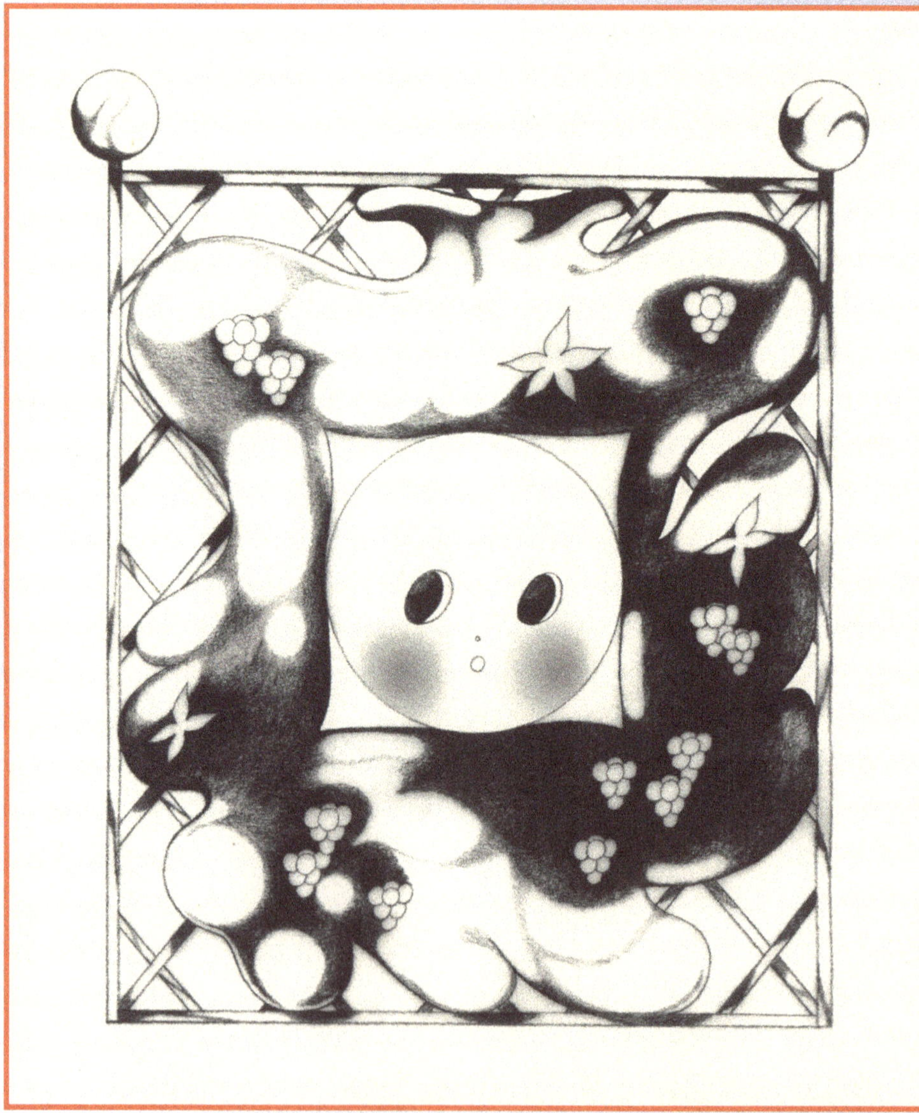

**summer fence**
GRAPHITE ON PAPER

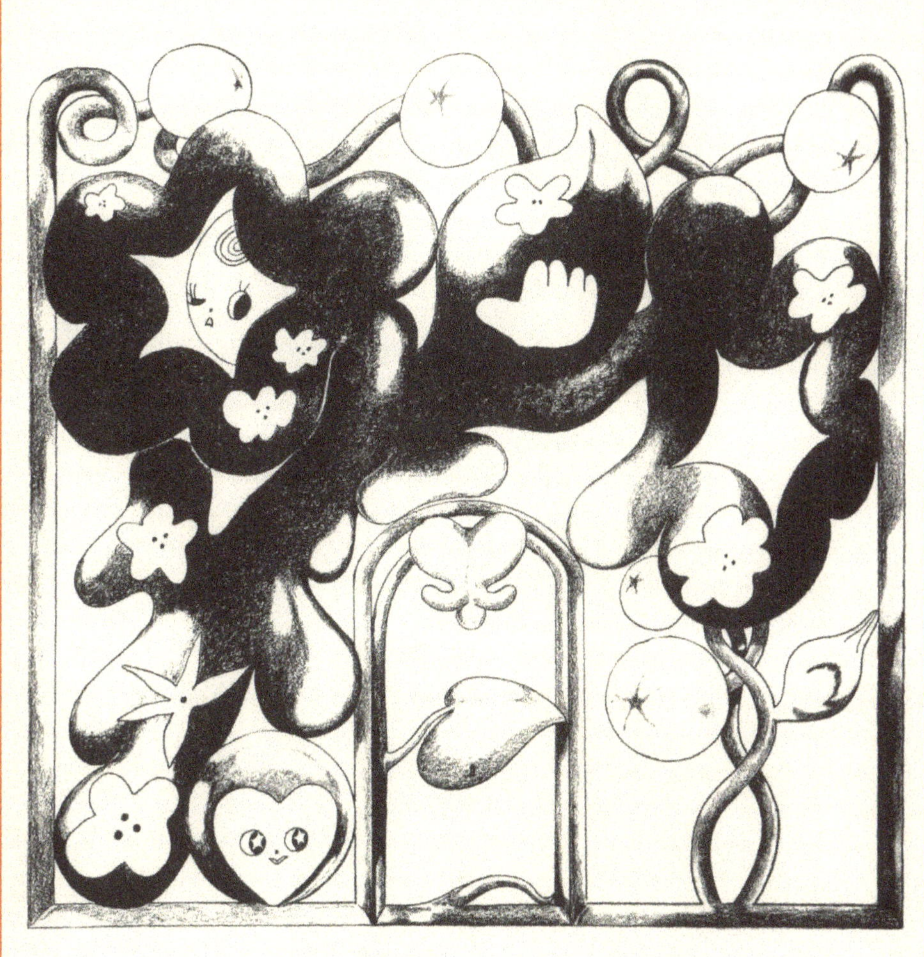

**unknown gate #2**
GRAPHITE ON PAPER

**Poetry by**
**Edie Koehlert**

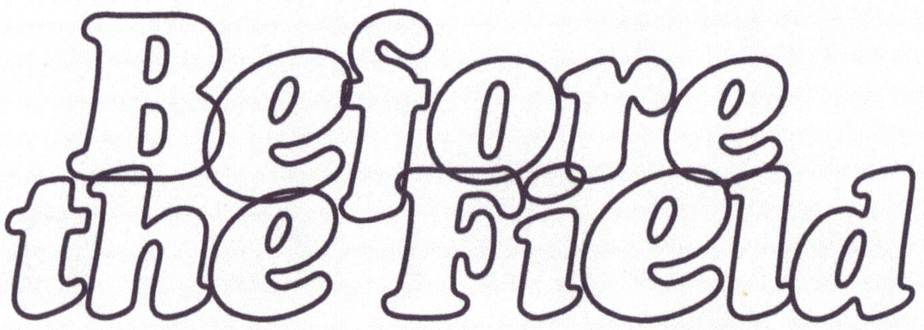

# Before the Field

Let's play that game. Do the twist. Lay in the morning and man-make the lake on the floor with small islands. Bask until the novelty of sensation wears off and then rub the face for a while. It's always got that same potency. Thin walls have nothing active in them, but she hears us and asks for quiet.

It's Friday morning, and how do you hold a gun? A woman inside you wants to kill a curled up man inside her. When she chokes him your breakneck heart-beat slows. It's a joke. You think you get to laugh at things. She touches steel to forehead. Everyone's keen on the thrill. On her turn she'll brush the trigger. Is that alright?

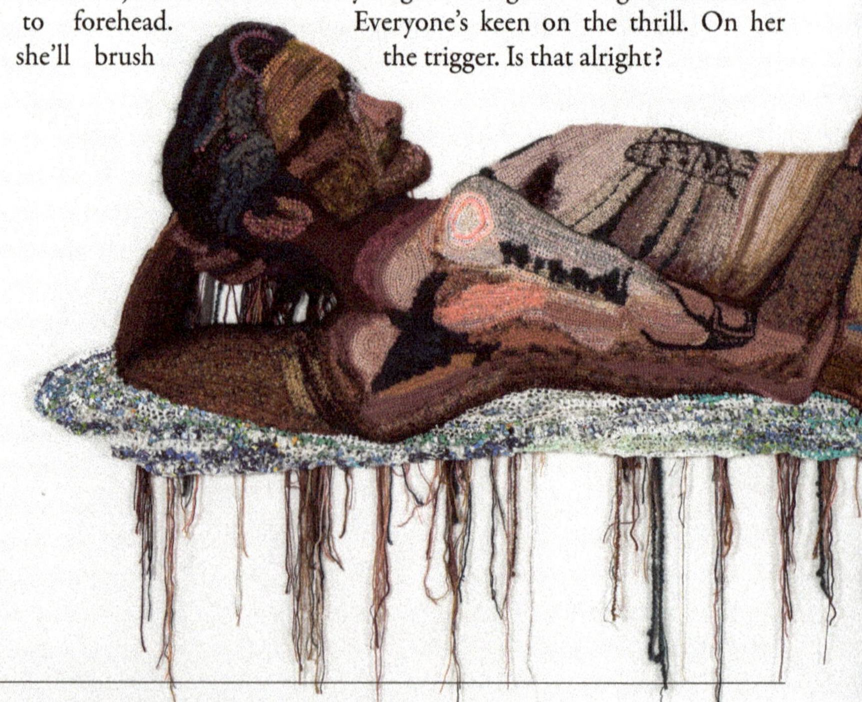

*Stratified Shining Island*
CROCHETED MIXED YARN AND UPCYCLED HOUSEHOLD PLASTIC

## *Textile by Jo Hamilton*

Ok now jerk and splay and actually contort because we're playing that game! Pleat the hair so it slides or at least so it leaves that thin residue on the scalp and back. Now leave home and slowly palm the flowers from the worst shrub in town. Consider the muscle of its drug.

Consider him smoking again and what that would do for his constitution. Tell him it wouldn't be good. Encourage him to be good. But really, it's easy to cheat the game. You get hungry, so you melt butter in a pan and mix it with cheese and milk. What would you dip in it? A sinuous protein of some kind, most likely. Take your turn Grown Up Mary Jelly Girl, fix your hair and right the inverted symbol you wear.

You tell him you wish for goddamn brunch! You wish for a mimosa and maybe a nice dress with spaghetti straps like you used to have when you went to the playground and liked the sprinklers! You wish for any comfort which made the small talk soft-boiled and laid the company out on the floor. But now people gather in the field to play humiliating games where girls and boys run from water. Fluid. Put you back so that the seeds may be sucked into the tree by their helicopter backs.

He wants to make his form inside you mean something. He says that he's inherent and resonant. And yes, there's a "you" and a "he". They are the same person looking at each other in the field for the first time. They're laughing, knowing the opposite of what the other says to be true. In unison now, *I am most interested in my mirror image and chokehold. I see you now. I want to play that game.* ✿

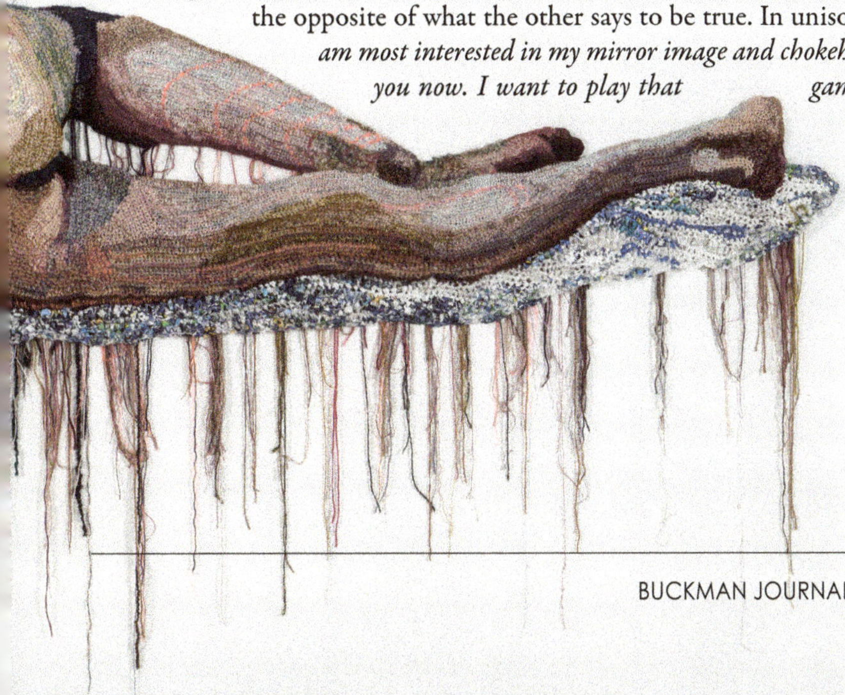

**Fiction by Lilly Grey Rudge**

# Buzzer

"Step forward now, on the X please. Why don't you tell us your name, age, and where you're from?"

I nod into the glaring spotlight, trying to focus on the four silhouettes behind the judges' table. The theater is much smaller than it seems on television, and it's hard not to glance at the six cameras positioned not fifteen feet from my face, stage light catching on their lenses.

"My name is Rainy, I'm twenty-one, and I'm from Ohio," I manage into the microphone.

"And is that a stage name?" The man's British accent adds to his otherwise uncharitable tone.

"Nope. You can even find it on my birth certificate." There is a pause, the audience unsure, until one of the producers holds up a hand, unleashing a tidal wave of overdone laughter.

"I guess I'm lucky though," I continue, "my parents being hippies paid off." This time the audience doesn't need a cue, and I notice that a few of the judges have cracked smiles of their own.

"Well, that remains to be seen, I suppose," the British man says, prompting a practiced eye roll from the blonde judge to his right.

"C'mon, Stew, give the girl the benefit of the doubt," she tells him, an elbow to his ribs. "I mean, look how cute she is!" She follows this with a wink in my direction that puts me at cardiovascular risk. Stew rolls his eyes but lets her admonish him, used to the schtick, as his finger reaches out to stroke the large red button in front of him. A single press will sound the buzzer and illuminate one of the gargantuan X's above the stage. Three X's and the audition is over. Three X's and I'm back to playing my most popular venue: the shower.

"Just ignore him sweetie," the blonde judge says to me, "He always has a stick up his ass."

"Hailee, watch the language

## *Printmaking by*
## Meagan Berlin

please," someone shouts from the edge of set, causing the judge to whip around in a blur of blonde extensions.

"You don't seem to mind the dickhead next to me swearing, so why don't you just edit it out?" There are a few coughs, an apology, and then she swivels to face the stage again. With a tight edit you would never know she'd been interrupted. "How about you ignore him and tell us what you'll be singing for us today?"

"It's an original." The strap of my guitar is rubbing a layer of skin from my neck. "I call it 'Starboard.'" Hailee nods, lifting a finger to brush her hidden earpiece, privy to a one-way conversation.

"Would you be open to changing the title?" she asks. My silence must stretch a moment too long because she asks again, voice a little louder this time.

"Yes. Yeah, totally, um… what do you think would be better?"

"Well we had better hear it first, yes?" Stew says. The audience laughs at my stupidity and lack of foresight. There are a few mumbled words between the judges and then a nod from Hailee, who, I assume, is my assigned ally. Only when the track begins do I lift the body of the guitar and feign pressing my fingers against the strings. I follow the chord progressions with muscle memory, plucking softly so I don't clash with the prerecorded accompaniment. I focus on my breathing as I deliver the first verse. It's impossible to read the crowd—not the judges' neatly shuttered expressions or the audience members' performative full-body sways—so I close my eyes.

The chorus is upbeat, bubbly, and I lift to my tiptoes, chasing each floating syllable as it leaves my mouth. Palms begin slapping together and I wonder if the judges are clapping along too. The song has caught me, carrying me along into the next verse and a higher register that shows off my range and, hopefully, lyrical prowess. I'm singing a few repetitive almost-rhymes, the crowd becoming familiar, now inches away from singing along when an echoing, guttural buzz slams me and bathes the stage in damning, stop-sign red. Stew has hit his button, his arms now crossed in a show of boredom. My fingers stutter against the strings but I plow on, suddenly thankful for the track still playing, unaffected, through the speakers. I miss the rest of the verse, swallowing down the acid crawling up my esophagus and pray they don't notice as I play catch up, hopping into the melody with an ill-timed crescendo. Any further mistakes are hidden by the blare of two more buzzers, this time from the bald man and dark-eyed woman, two judges who have yet to speak. This, finally, is enough to end the track, my mouth snapping shut.

> "I'M SINGING A FEW REPETITIVE ALMOST-RHYMES, THE CROWD BECOMING FAMILIAR, NOW INCHES AWAY FROM...

> ...SINGING ALONG WHEN AN ECHOING, GUTTURAL BUZZ SLAMS ME AND BATHES THE STAGE IN DAMNING, STOP-SIGN RED."

"Well, Rainy, first let's talk about what I like about you," Stew says, pen pressed against his bottom lip. "You've got the look. I could tell the moment you stepped out here—you look like you could be a pop star."

I know that he's referring to my haircut, a fashionable shag based on a two-minute tutorial, and the dark lace dress I borrowed from my roommate and hemmed to brush the tops of my knees. The way his eyes comb over my body, though, suggests more than a skin-deep evaluation.

He continues, "The song was fine. Not great but not bad. Just not interesting enough for me to want to hear the rest." There are a few well-timed boos from the crowd.

Hailee is next, offering similar compliments and calling me cute again, to which Stew shakes his head. "We're not looking for cute though, are we?" he butts in. "We're looking for what's going to be hot." There are murmurs of agreement from the two other judges, who lean forward, eager to pile on.

"I've got to agree with Stew," the other female judge announces into her microphone, "which I never thought I'd say." She is British too, a founding member of some girl group that never quite made it in the states. "You've got a nice voice and seem like a sweet girl, but the presence isn't quite there. To be frank, I just wish there were more of you to fill up the stage." I smile like she has given me a compliment, aware of the increasing zoom on the camera to my left.

"I see what Del and Stew are saying," the bald man finally chimes in. "There's something missing. I'm not convinced you're totally aware of your identity as an artist."

"Oh and you were at her age, Hank?" Hailee leans forward, fully committed to her role as my advocate, a move which has Hank raising his arms in a sign of defeat.

"All I'm saying is we're not exactly looking for another solo artist," he says, making eye contact with Stew across the table. "You know what's hot right now? Groups. She's got a good group look to her. She could be the folksy one. Or the angry one. Do you often get angry?"

"Um, not really."

"Ever scream into a mic?"

"Not yet..."

"Ever smash a guitar?"

"That's off the point," Stew, my unlikely hero, interrupts. "But I don't entirely disagree." His eyes return to mine for the first time since the start of the judges' deliberation. "Would you be open to it?"

"To—to smashing my guitar?" This time the responding laughter is genuine. Even Stew grins, almost like he's grown fond of me.

"Please don't, not on my stage." Another round of audience cackles. "No, I mean would you be open to being in a group?" If there is an insult in his question, he does a surprisingly good job of hiding it. Hailee is nodding at me earnestly, willing the next words to come from my mouth.

"Sure, I'd be open to it." *I'll try anything once* teeters at the tip of my tongue, but I remember I'm on network television and opt for an awkward thumbs up.

"Great, let's make it happen." Stew waves for the show's host—a tall, C-list celebrity with an Invisalign brand deal, one of Hollywood's hundred Chrises—who appears at my elbow to lead me offstage. I can't tell if this is a permanent dismissal and looking back at the judges is no help—Del has already disappeared, Stew is talking to a producer, and both Hailee and Hank are scrolling their phones with glazed eyes.

Chris whisks me into the cavernous backstage area. He points me towards what looks like a photobooth. "Film your post-audition interview and come out when you're done." I nod, turning towards the booth when he stops me with another light touch. "Wait, before that, give me your hand."

I notice he is wearing gloves.

They are powder blue and clash terribly with his suit, more appropriate for a dentist than the reality personality taking hold of my hand. He turns it palm up, ensuring each of my fingers are spread evenly apart before pulling something that looks like a stubby pen from his jacket. Placing its tip to the pad of my ring finger, he clicks a button. When I try to shake the pain away, blood drips to the floor.

"Jesus, what was that for?"

"You can go ahead to the interview," he says, turning on his heel to disappear back into the wings before I have a chance to protest. I can feel my heartbeat in my hand as I shuffle into the booth, which is larger and brighter than I'd expected. There is a band-aid waiting for me on the chair.

The interview goes quickly, a robotic voice asking me questions about the judges' critiques as I stare into a one-way mirror that I know hides a lens. It's not hard to fall into autopilot, offering the same phrases I practiced in my own bathroom mirror. By the time the final questions come, I'm answering in an easy rhythm:

"Do you give the network and its affiliates permission to use you for the formation of a trademarked musical and entertainment group, yes or no?"

"Yes."

"Do you give the network and its affiliates permission to compensate you as an individual rather than a larger organized entity, yes or no?"

"Yes."

"Do you give the network and its affiliates permission to use and duplicate your name, likeness, biometric data, and genome for entertainment and promotional purposes, yes or no?"

"Oh, um, would you mind repeating that one?" I shift slightly, the backs of my thighs sticking to the pleather chair.

"Yes or no?" the voice repeats.

"If you could repeat the whole thing, I didn't quite get it all." My reflection is starting to look flustered and I smooth a hand over my hair.

"Yes or no?"

"I mean, yes, but I just want to make sure I understand—"

"Thank you. Group formation initiating." There is a click and the lights of the booth dim. The interview is over. Chris is waiting for me outside.

"All done? Great, follow me." He leads me deeper backstage, making one-sided conversation as I struggle to keep up. "It's nice that they've made all the bureaucratic consent stuff verbal now, isn't it?" he says, long legs completing one step for each of my three. "No more paper contracts or signatures, it speeds everything up."

"Where are we going?" I ask, trying not to huff and puff. If Chris notices my lack of physical fitness, he does not comment or slow down.

"The other girls should be here in the next couple minutes," he tells me, stopping abruptly in front of an unmarked dressing room door. "You can wait here until they're ready."

Swinging the door open, he ushers me inside and points me toward a makeup chair flanked by two others, already occupied.

"Oh good, looks like a couple of them are already waiting for you," Chris says. "Introduce yourselves and I'll be back with the rest. I'm sure you'll have plenty in common." He barks out a laugh and swings the door shut behind him, rattling the mirrors lining the wall. Settling into my seat, I use the reflection across from us to steal a glance at one of my neighbors. Her hair is dark like mine, cut into a pixie, and there is already a heavy layer of foundation over her face that makes her look a bit like a department store mannequin. There is something familiar about the shape of her face—the slight cleft of her chin and crease between her eyebrows. She bites her bottom lip and I catch a glimpse of her front teeth, one slightly overlapping the other. My tongue bumps across my own.

"SHE BITES HER BOTTOM LIP AND I CATCH A GLIMPSE OF HER FRONT TEETH, ONE SLIGHTLY OVERLAPPING THE OTHER. MY TONGUE BUMPS ACROSS MY OWN."

The other girl is uncannily similar, with a different, longer haircut. It isn't until they both return my stare that I realize I've been looking back and forth between them, all subtlety thrown to the wind.

"Sorry, um, I'm Rainy. Are you both members of 'the group?'" I use air quotes, hoping to lighten the vibe between us. The twins seem confused, trading looks with one another. "Oh, well, have you already auditioned?"

"Yes," they say simultaneously.

"Okay, cool." I try to relax my posture slightly, unsure when I became wound this tightly. "Sorry, have we met before? You just seem really familiar. What are your names?"

The sisters are properly slack-jawed now, like I've asked them their social security number or blood type.

"Or, you don't have to tell me if you don't want to...did you just audition?"

"Yes," they say simultaneously and I can't help but jump in my seat. Because it's more than the word that is the same. It's their intonation and the way they tilt their heads, a slight lift to both of their voices as they study me in the mirror.

"And they...they asked you to be in a group?"

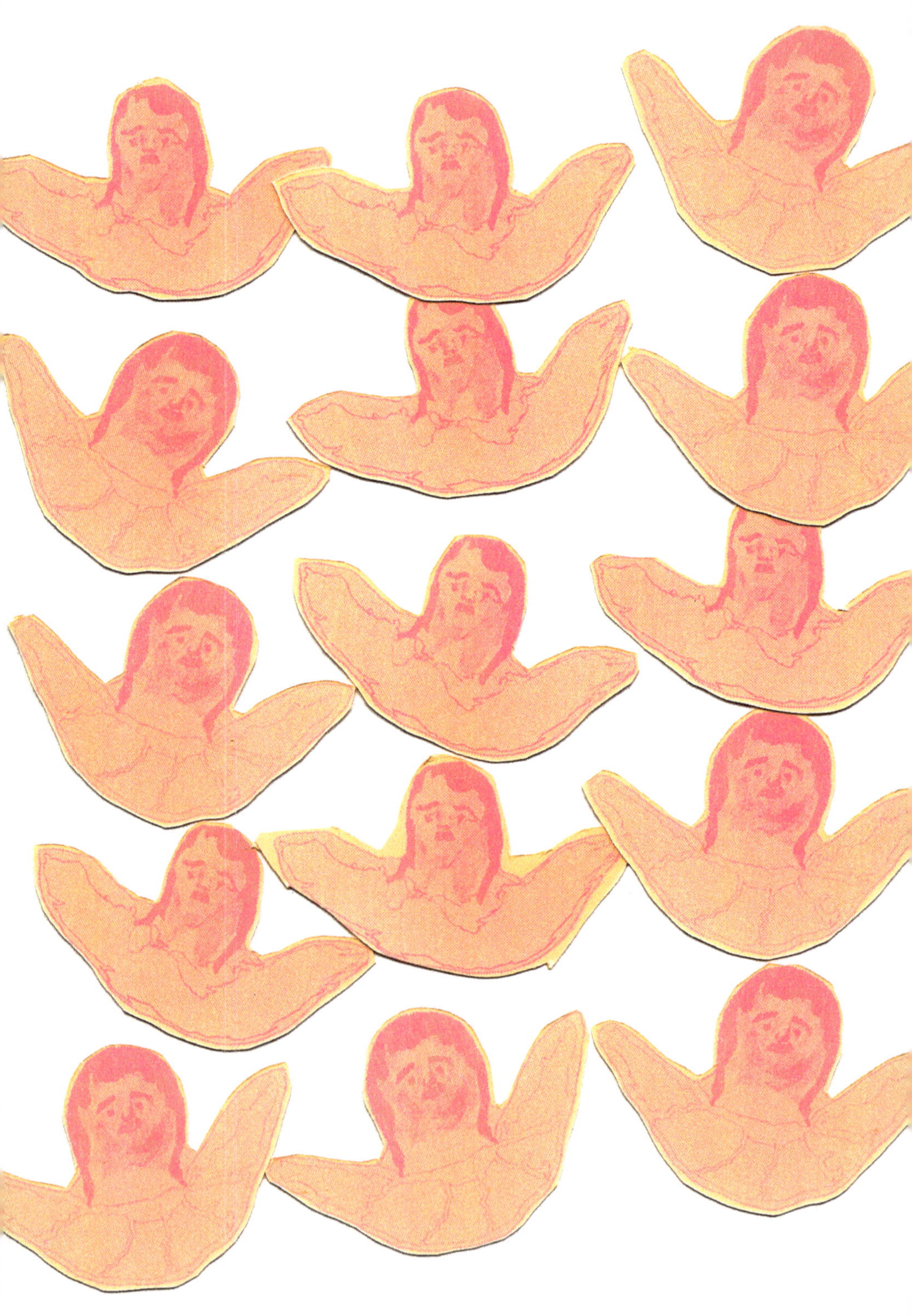



*vesnyanky ii*
PENCIL DRAWING PRINTED WITH RISOGRAPH

This time they don't bother confirming, instead turning their heads to look back into the mirror. I do the same, trying not to swallow my tongue as I take in the triplets staring back at me.

When Chris comes in I'm on the other side of the room, curled on a couch that probably costs more than my rent. There are two more girls with him—another pair of lookalikes, this time with colorful hair setting them apart. The purple one takes what was my seat at the mirror, while the red one sits next to the pixie cut, who has finally finished her makeup in a style reminiscent of my senior prom photos. Somehow she makes it look sexy.

"All right ladies, you're on in ten. Make sure you're in the outfits we've provided." Chris says briskly. There is a flutter of affirmatives. I sink deeper into the couch.

"I know it's a little disorienting," Chris says as he slides in next to me, "But you should start getting ready. They'll go on with or without you." Purple comes out first, her dress the same color as her hair.

"How'd you have time to dye their hair?" I remain in my seat and Chris sighs.

"I don't understand all the sciencey parts of it, but they don't even have to dye it. They just change a couple bits of DNA before they run it through the system, and boom, black hair turns to purple."

"So they aren't really me, then?" I've realized it as I've been studying them, in those long minutes between deserting my chair and Chris's return. Even without makeup they lack the hyperpigmentation that surrounds my own eyes like a raccoon. Their noses seem straighter than mine, their eyes brighter. Even their complexions are warmer and less pasty. "They just seem a little more..."

"Talented, attractive, spunky, ethnically ambiguous? Let's just say we made them more marketable. And you too. All this," he gestures to the dressing room and the four dolled-up women now leaning in wait against the mirror, "comes from you. You're still the main ingredient." I stare back, eyes wide. "Just go with it. Trust me. Do you think I was ready to be a star the first time around?"

I allow myself to really study him. His angular nose, clear skin, and, now that he's said it, ethnically ambiguous features. Even with a gun to my head I'm not sure I would be able to guess his age. "And now?" I ask him.

"Now what?"

"Are you ready to be a star?" The smile he offers me belongs on one of his Invisalign billboards.

He moves to stand, gesturing toward the door. "Well, it looks like the others have already made their decision," he says, reaching out to pluck the last costume from the rack. It practically floats from his hand into a silky pile on my lap. "I suggest you make yours within the next two minutes."

"Ladies and gentlemen, please welcome to the stage, The Rainys!" We file out in a straight line, falling into step before taking our places across the X. The judges don't ask for an introduction. Instead, Stew leans forward and says, short and clipped into his microphone, "Go ahead."

I didn't think to grab my guitar, so when the track begins I'm left wringing my hands and counting the bars until the first verse. The rest of the group appears to be similarly thrown off, our straight line quickly becoming a blob as we shift around the stage searching for some kind of formation. Red Rainy brushes her shoulder against mine, making me wobble and almost miss the start of the verse, but I balance myself just in time to start singing. At first I think the other girls have forgotten the words; it's only my voice emanating from the stage, powerful and precise, but then the harmonies begin and I'm caught in the rising tide of our vocals, almost identical, weaving around each other with flowing precision. We understand the capabilities of each group member, their range and dynamics, because they are one in the same. Our bodies, our voices, even the mind that wrote these lyrics—we all understand them with perfect, lived experience. We are moving together now, anticipating each step. I can see the judges' fingers twitching, desperate for a reason to press their buzzers, to pull the stage and our future out from beneath us. We don't give them one.

"I CAN SEE THE JUDGES' FINGERS TWITCHING, DESPERATE FOR A REASON TO PRESS THEIR BUZZERS...

...TO PULL THE STAGE AND OUR FUTURE OUT FROM BENEATH US. WE DON'T GIVE THEM ONE."

The last of my breath is stolen as the track fades and the audience leaps to their feet, their applause deafening and unprompted by producers. It takes a full minute for it to fade to a dull roar and even longer to get them back in their seats. The response from the judges isn't quite as enthusiastic, save for Hailee, but they offer us their own slow, celebratory claps and wizened nods. They saw this coming, after all. Once again, Stew kicks things off.

"Now *that* was a memorable performance. What did I tell you?"

The Rainys laugh and pixie cut Rainy shoots finger guns in his direction. "I knew you had it in you."

"Talk about memorable, I won't be able to get your faces out of my head!" Hank exclaims, slamming a palm against the table. "It's like copy, paste, copy, paste, all across the stage. If I didn't like you so much, I'd say it's unsettling."

"You can say that again," Del chimes in. "I mean I'm all for being in sync but you all take it to another level. I've got to admit," she continues, cheating out to the nearest camera, "while your similarities are a strength, I'm worried they could also be a weakness."

"See, I was thinking that too. I worry about too much of the same, you know?" Hank pauses and takes a sip of his soda, unable to articulate further. The group is still following along, our simultaneous nods doing little to disprove his point.

"What do you think, Stew?" Del asks. Stew is raking his gaze down the line of Rainys.

"Well you're not going to believe me when I say this, but I think I agree with the panel." There are a few hoots throughout the auditorium while Hank feigns a heart attack. "I know, I know, I hate to say it. But when it comes to Hollywood, what we really value is originality."

I keep my smile in place even as his words hit me like a leaden ball. "What I'm wondering is," he continues, eyes narrowing, "which of you is the original? Who is the trendsetter? Who is the main ingredient of this group?" My lips come apart, eager to answer, to raise my hand, to jump off the stage and approach the table until they are forced to remember me and my real, authentic, imperfect face. But Stew raises a finger.

"So, what do you think?" he asks, turning to the judges. "Hailee, you're their biggest fan. Who on this stage is the star we've been looking for?"

Hailee rolls her eyes but appears to take the question seriously, scanning the Rainys, left to right, until she zeroes in on someone. Lifting a hand, she points. "That one."

"Far left?" Del asks.

"Yes, her."

"I agree," Stew says, "and that's all that really matters, isn't it?" Cue laughter. "Would you step forward please? No, no, not you. You, with the short hair." Pixie cut Rainy steps forward into a newly illuminated spotlight. "Can you tell us your name, age, and where you're from?"

"My name is Rainy, I'm twenty-one, and I'm from Ohio."

"Well, Rainy, I've got good news for you. I think you're a star," he says, planting his elbows firmly on the judges' table. "Would you be open to going solo?" ✿

# So

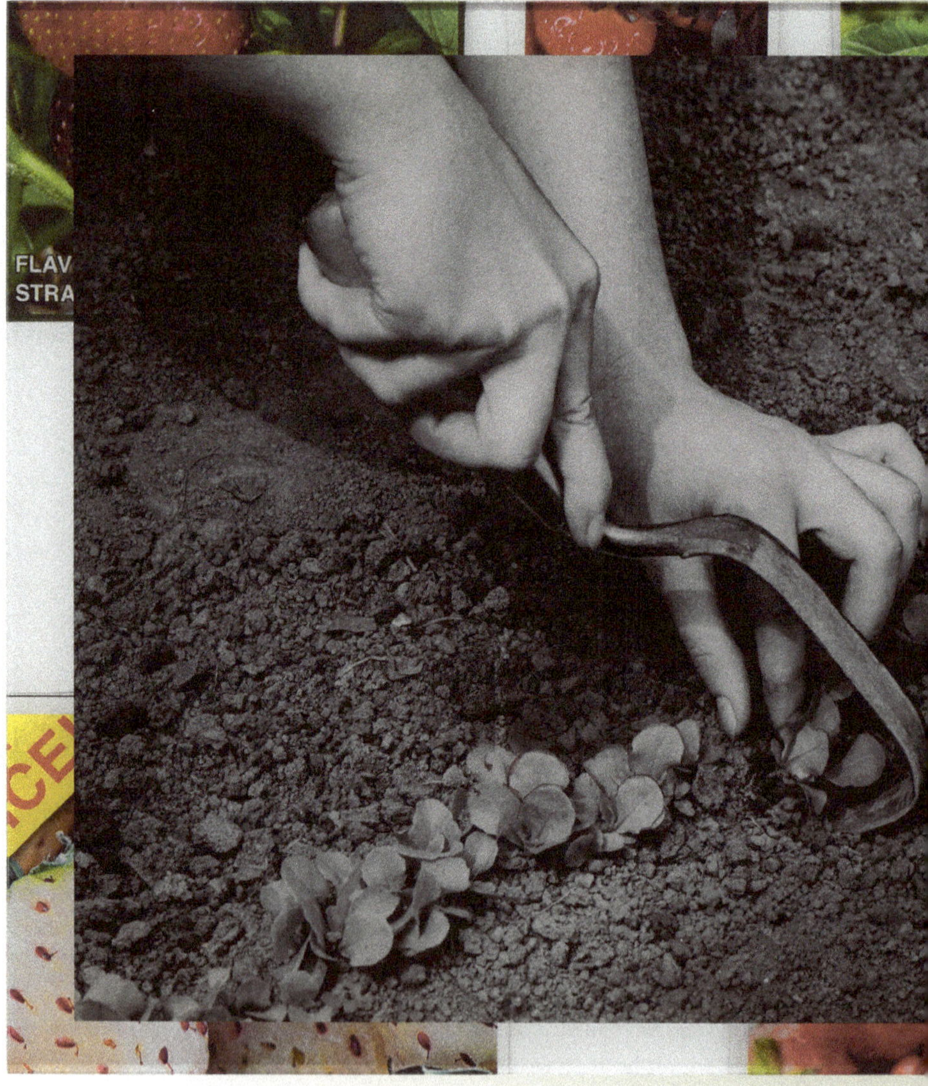


## *Mixed Media by*
## **Sarah Meadows**

 *Persistence I*
ARCHIVAL PIGMENT PRINT MOUNTED TO DIBOND AND PLEXIGLASS

# Much So

The year I was at my most reckless
I lived on Quarry St.
It neither killed me
nor made me stronger
There's a way that a smaller envelope
can get lost inside of a larger envelope
That's how it was

Sitting next to you on the train
or in the theater
I thrummed
like 500 French Verbs
I was prepared to get on my hands and knees
and crawl for it, understudy to the nightshade that I was
The last conversation we had
stayed with me

A photograph without its punctum
A ladder left up all night

***Poetry by***
**Harper Quinn**

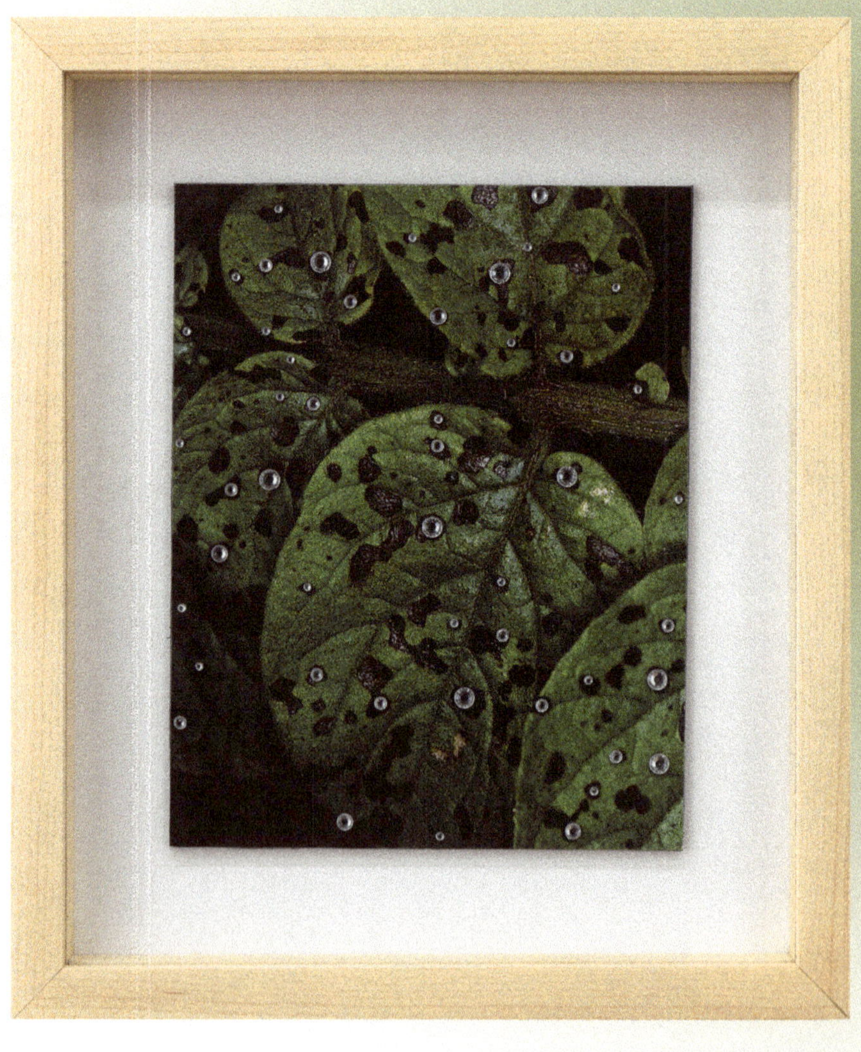

126 *Early Blight*
ARCHIVAL PIGMENT PRINT AND SELF-ADHESIVE RHINESTONES IN A MAPLE FRAME

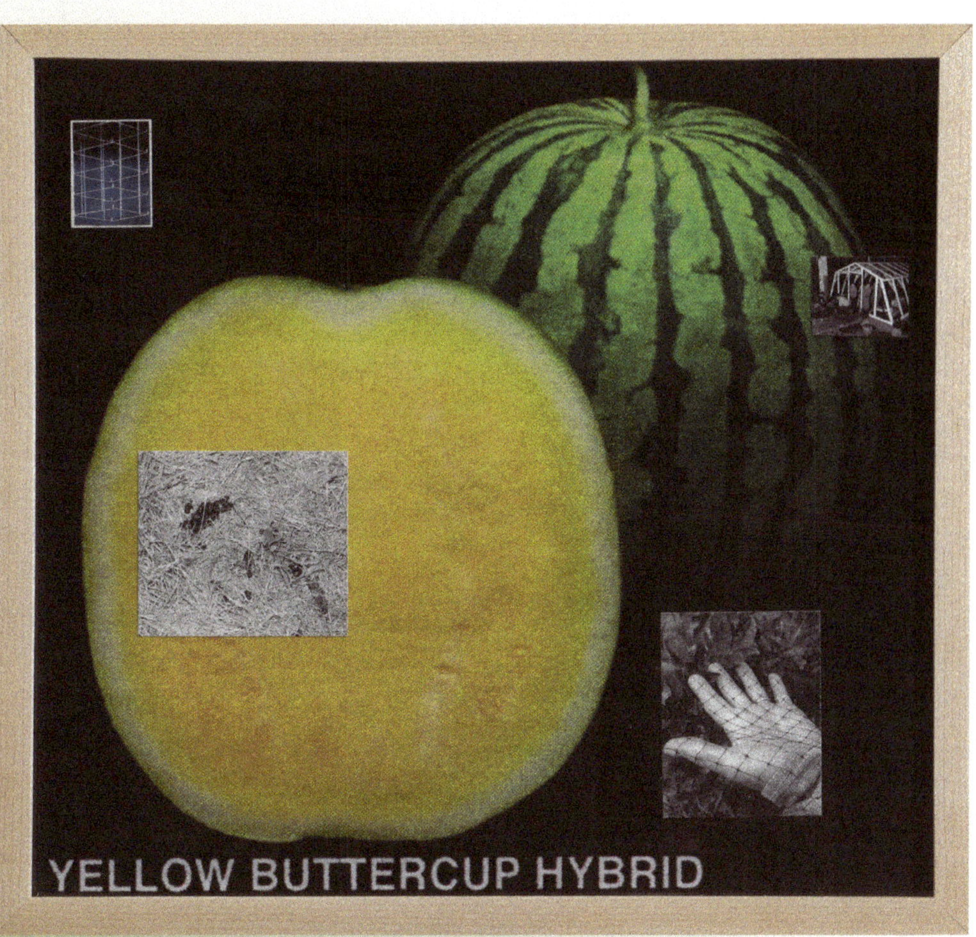


*Buttercup Hybrid*
ARCHIVAL PIGMENT PRINTS AND LASER PRINTS IN A MAPLE FRAME

# CONTRIBUTORS

Joon Ae Haworth-Kaufka (she/they) is a co-founder of the reading series Constellation, VOICES, a BIPOC Adoptee Community, and Yeondae, a now-retired social justice collective of Asian adoptees. She is a 2024 Oregon Humanities storytelling fellow, and a 2025 recipient of an Asian American Journalists Association award.

JOONAEHK.COM

IG @JOONAE.HK

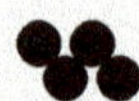

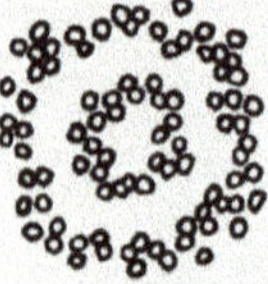

After several years in advertising, Pearlyn Tan (she/her) found the work unfulfilling and chose to pursue a more meaningful creative path. In 2016, she began drawing under a metonym on Instagram as a way to navigate the emotional landscape of new motherhood.

PEARLYN.NET

IG @THE_UNORDINARY_MOTHERHOOD

Michael Kurt (he/him) is a former industrial musician, and a current writer, photographer, and playwright. He is the co-editor of *Berm*, a contemporary arts magazine based in Portland.

IG @MICHAELPRODUCT

Hannah Krafcik (they/them) has been taking dance classes since they were five years old as a way to satiate sensory needs and bodymind curiosities. A neuroqueer love of pattern recognition, which in turn helps to locate connections, is central to Krafcik's art practice.

HANNAHKRAFCIK.COM

IG @HANNAHKELIZA

After working in Chicago, New Delhi, and New York as a journalist, writer, and editor, Torea Frey (she/they) returned to Oregon and transitioned to visual art. She is interested in ephemeral things, obsolete media, and ways of resisting transactional productivity-related pursuits.

TOREAFREY.COM

IG @TOREAJADE

Will A.C. Mulligan (he/him) is an environmental consultant, banjo player, and lifelong West Coaster who writes poetry, often working in the ekphrastic tradition of responding to visual art with poems.

WILLACMULLIGAN.COM

Ruby Wang (she/they) is a Chinese-American Scorpio fiction writer who recently matriculated in the masters program at UMass Amherst.

RUBYWANG.CARRD.CO

Ari Albertson (they/them) works primarily with sculpture and sound. Their current work explores the dancefloor as a site of analog experience of flow, collective embodiment, and somatosensory engagement.

ARIALBERTSON.WORDPRESS.COM

IG @AALBLYNN

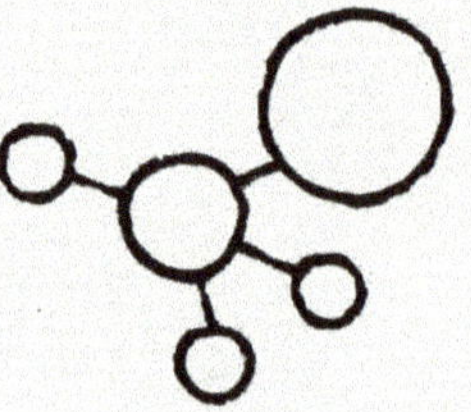

Karl Anderson (he/him) is an artist and writer exploring themes of obsolescence, communication, and informational exchange. Employing salvage and the creative repurposing of technology, Karl's work often appears in the form of under-the-radar installations in exterior public spaces.

FUTEL.NET

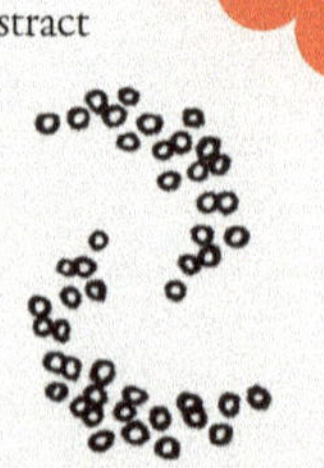

Inspired by the history of color, poetry, and cinematic compositions, Kristen Diederich (she/her) developed her abstract landscape painting style during periods of time spent in coastal Maine, Oregon, and Europe.

KRISTENDIEDERICH.COM

IG @KDIEDERICHSTUDIO

When not hopping between mediums, Bell Mayrer (she/her) spends a lot of time imagining how plants talk to each other, and mapping out an imaginary garden. Bell makes comics and believes in books as objects that can be held, carried, and shared.
ARABELLAMAYRER.COM
IG @ARABELLA_EM

Dan Gluibizzi (he/him) lives with his wife, daughter and two cats. Most days, Dan is drawing and painting in his backyard studio in SE Portland.
IG @DANGLUIBIZZI

After city hopping on the West Coast and wearing many hats, Dana Cera (she/her) has acquired much grist for the writing mill; she is currently writing a memoir in scenes entitled *Graceland is Open Daily*.
DANAHERENOW.SUBSTACK.COM

Rowan Tate (she/her) is a Romanian creative and curator. She reads nature books, the backs of shampoo bottles, and sometimes minds.

After graduating from the Glasgow School of Art in the 1990s, Jo Hamilton (she/her) moved to Portland where she integrated years of drawing and painting with handcraft learned from her grandmother. Her work is primarily made from post-consumer materials.
JOHAMILTONART.COM
IG @JOHAMILTONART

Kirsten Merrell Kippen (she/her) was raised in Alaska and has lived in Portland for 20 years. She loves exploring Forest Park, and frequenting North Portland libraries. Merrell Kippen lives with her sculptor husband, artist daughters, and golden retriever named Ozma.

Through sculptural, painterly, and temporal processes, Nicholas Moler-Gallardo (he/him) creates fragmented splendor that emerges from the normal and known.
NICHOLASMOLER-GALLARDO.COM
IG @MOLER_GALLARDO

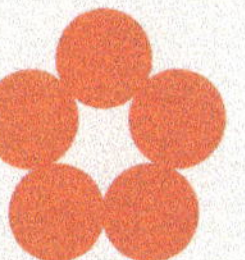

Kaya Noteboom (she/her) writes fiction, cultural criticism, and is at work on a collection of essays about the literary craft of self-annihilation.

Georgia Phipps (she/her) enjoys textile crafts, junk journaling, and spending time with her cats Yuki and Susu. Phipps doesn't sell or promote her artwork but loves making things for friends and family. Aggregate, the word, and the title of her piece means "a group of things assembled without tight organization, but still forming a cohesive whole."

Milo R. Muise (they/them) is finishing up an essay collection exploring the (sometimes overlapping) roles of fantasy in transmasculinity, eroticism, and mental illness. When not writing or puzzling, they're watching movies with their dog, Rigatoni Collette.
MILO-MUISE.COM
IG @MILO_MILO_MILO

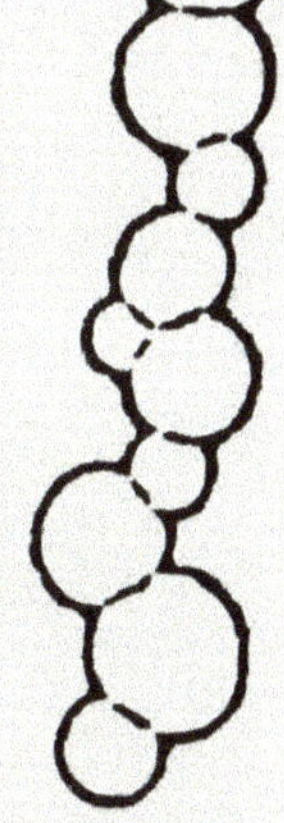

Jenene Nagy (she/her) is a visual artist whose work is held in several permanent collections across the country. Previous residencies include Yaddo and the Sitka Center for Art + Ecology. She is a former foster youth, first-generation college grad, and lives with a poodle and a tortoise, Buttercup.
@PDXCONTEMPORARYART
#JENENENAGY

Thea Prieto (she/her) is the author of *From the Caves*, a speculative novella about a group of future cave-dwelling humans and the stories they live by. She teaches creative writing at various higher learning institutions in Portland.
THEAPRIETO.COM
IG @THEA.PRIETO

Rachel Warkentin (she/her) is a ceramics artist, painter, and owner of Barrow PDX, a local jewelry brand. She grew up "in the kind of nowhere between Portland and the coast." Although working in many different mediums, she always returns to oil paint, egg tempera, and clay. Her cat is named Sister Bruce.

IG @RACHWARK

Maxwell Kline is an artist and writer raised and currently growing in the Pacific Northwest. Maxie co-organizes the Graft Union Reading Series and is working on a new edition of Carmilla, available soon through First Wound.

MAXIE.RODEO

Although residing in Portland, Emma Riskin (she/her) credits the California coast and its horizon as a major influence in her writing, which sifts through desire, permission, and liberation.

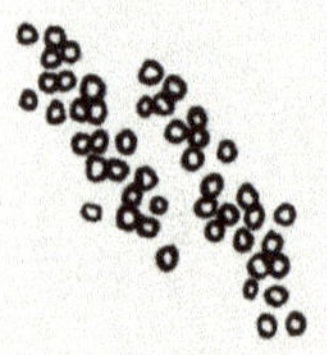

Noah Jordan (he/him) lives in Portland, and is working on his first novel. Noah also edits *Welcome Editorial*.

@NNOAHAONN

NOAHJORDAN.SUBSTACK.COM

Taylor Wallau (any pronouns) works as a substitute in Portland Public Schools, which allows flexibility to devote time to the anti-capitalist pursuits of radical printmaking, creative writing, mutual aid, and anti-imperialist struggle. Wallau's practice is also influenced by the somatic healing arts, astrology, tarot, and animistic traditions.

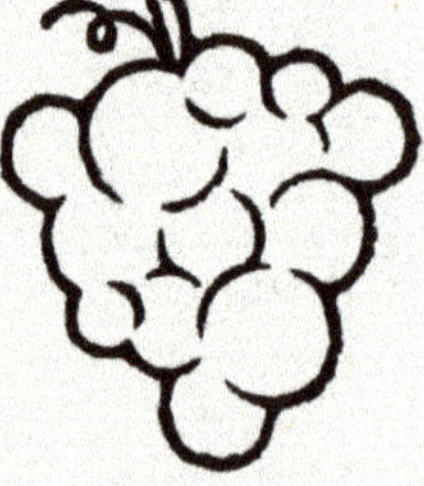

TAYLOR-WALLAU.SQUARESPACE.COM

IG @PRACTICE_REBELLION

Josh Cox (he/they) offers no biographical insight other than his poems.

Ocean (he/him) is a disabled poet, novelist, and visual artist residing in the lush muck at the southern extent of the Salish Sea. He is currently the Poet Laureate of Olympia, Washington.

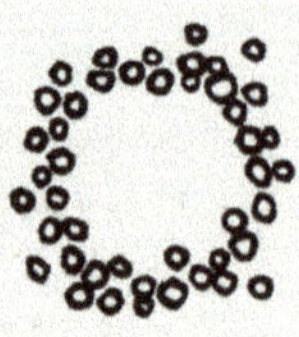

MIRRORFLOWER.ORG

IG @MIRRORFLOWER_OCEAN

Edie Koehlert (she/her) is a creative writing student who champions new blood in the Portland literary scene through the Graft Union Reading Series.

IG @EDIEKOE

Lilly Grey Rudge (she/her) wrote her first short story at nine years old, which featured an alarming amount of disembowelment. She continues to write the odd and macabre and play existential board games.

Meagan Berlin (they/them) is a printmaker, illustrator, and tattoo artist working in the territories of the Lək̓ʷəŋən peoples (Victoria, BC). Some of their personal creative projects include making mobiles, pysanky, and playing with their scanner.

BERLINILLUSTRATION.COM

BERLINTATTOOS.COM

IG @BERLIN.TATTOOS

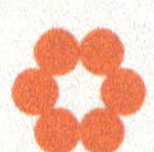

Sarah Meadows (she/her) is an Oregon-based visual artist and film photographer published by the Institute for Interspecies Art & Relations. She is a collector of archival images interested in the overlap of nature, poetry, and history.

SARAH-MEADOWS.COM

IG @SMEADOWSMEADOWS

Harper Quinn (she/they) incorporates printmaking, bookarts, letter-writing, and collage into their poetic process. She lives in Portland, Oregon and is part of the staff leadership collective at the Independent Publishing Resource Center.

HARPERQUINN.COOL

# HONOR ROLL

***Charlie King***
**Chuck Kesey**
***D'Angelo***
**Isaka Shamsud-Din**
***Jane Goodall***
**June Sanregret**
***Justin Woodward***
**Kerry Hunt**
***Portland Fruit Tree Project***
**Rosalyn Drexler**
***Sue Kesey***
**Terry Voss**

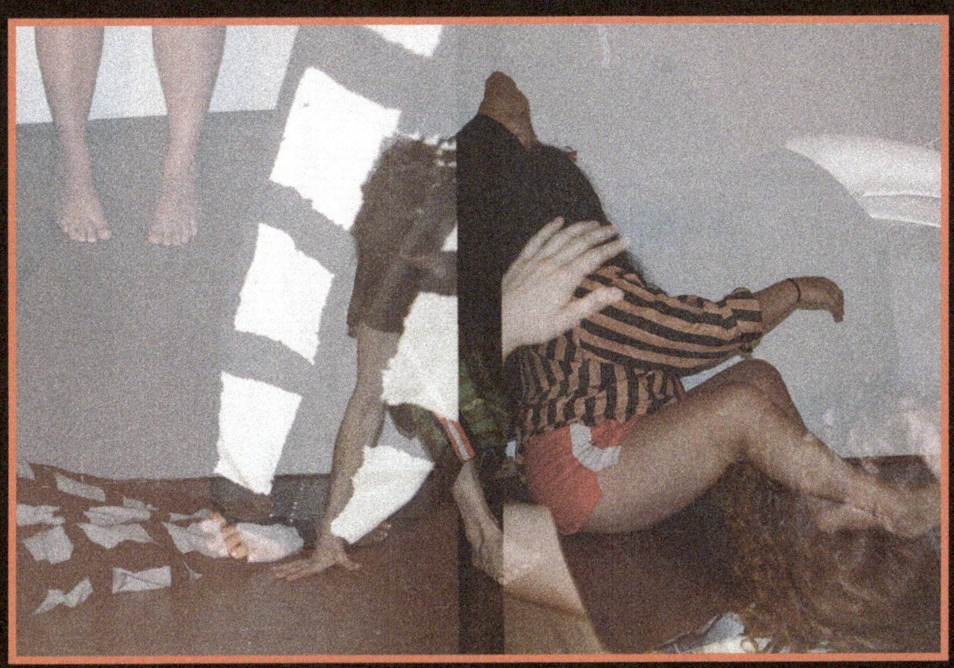

# MORE FROM BUCKMVN

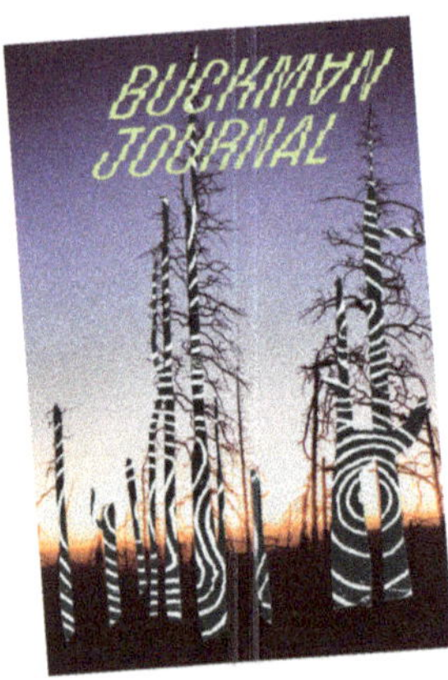


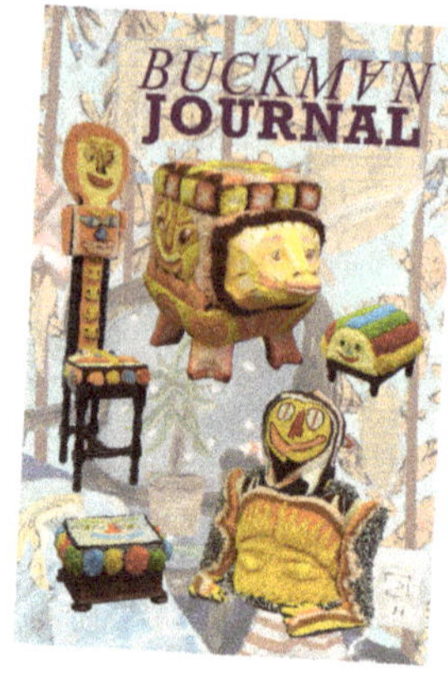


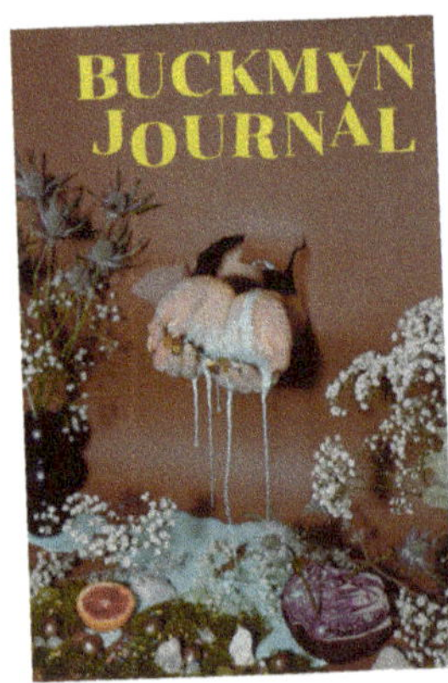


## Other journals

*Buckman Journal* is a vehicle. An anthology inspired by and made to showcase Portland's literary and artistic talent. Each biannual issue collects the creativity at work in our city and packs full-color pages with the work of over 25 local writers and artists across all genres. Open one up and find everything from poems to recipes to essays, photography, painting, sculpture, collage, and beyond. Stories of action, humor, and wonder are paired with page-leaping art. Award-winning authors and eye dazzles abound in Buckman. With a recognition from the Independent Publishers Book Awards, *Buckman Journal* is here to keep print media alive and kicking.

## Know your local!

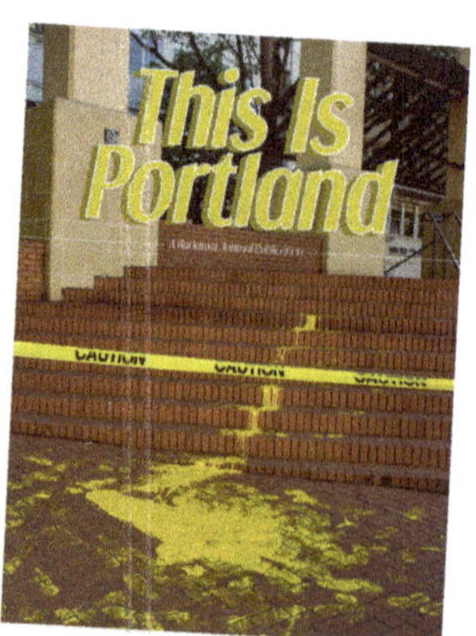


Finally! A real dose of Portland, and who better to deliver it than some of the city's most respected artists, writers, shakers, and doers. A travel book can tell you where to eat and sleep, but *This is Portland* conveys the city's soul and spirit more faithfully than any other. Contributors include Michelle Ruiz Keil (Ursula K. Le Guin Prize for Fiction Finalist), Pace Taylor (*NY Times*), Chris Stuck (Pushcart Prize winner, Amistad/HarperCollins), Scott Korb (*New Yorker*), Lauren Yoshiko (*Broccoli*), Erin Nations (Eisner and Ignatz nominated), and many more. Short stories. Essays. Comics. Poetry. Recipes. Photos. Painting. Tarot. Illustrations. Mixed Art. Presented in a GIANT paperback book.

# Most recent title

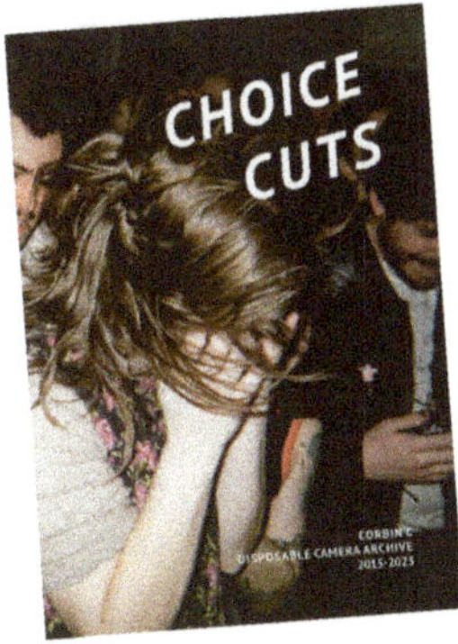


A raucous concert in a stranger's basement. People in the thick of a downtown Portland protest. A cat convention at the airport Holiday Inn. *Choice Cuts: Disposable Camera Archive 2015-2023* by Corbin C dives into these local scenes and beyond. The book offers a lively montage of Portland, Oregon and its long-running traditions of hosting bands in homes and making space for the strange. Captured entirely with single-use disposable cameras, the photographs echo the DIY spirit of the communities they document.

# Other titles

*The Night You Were Born* by Bronmin Shumway
*Odd Guide to the Flowers of Portland*
*Cornfry* by Rich Perin
*The Pinnacle* by Benjamin Kessler
*Hal* by Amanda Berlind
*Rain or Coincidences* by Xinyu Liu
*Many Seasons* by Frances Badalamenti
*Somewhere in Another Place* by Mike Vos
*In the Frail* by Erinn Kathryn
*The Great Gatsby: Buckman Critical Edition*
*Metamorphic Door* by Carolyn Supinka
*Tiny Haiku* by Daniel O'Brien-Bravi
*Fish Cough* by Craig Buchner
*What We Pick Up* by Stacy Brewster
*The Scream & Other Dark Stories* by Jerry Sampson
*The Last Payphone on the West Coast* by Rich Perin
*Another Fortune & Other Poems* by Elizabeth Rivers
*20!8: The Order of Athena vs. The Orange Bastard* by Anita Lobo
*The Right Tool & Other Poor Choices* by Craig Foster

All these titles, and more, can be found at buckmanjournal.com. You can also find our titles at any local reputable bookstore or in our book vending machines around town.

www.ingramcontent.com/pod-product-compliance
Lightning Source LLC
Chambersburg PA
CBHW050032040726
47599CB00015B/1639

* 9 7 8 1 9 6 7 0 5 8 0 5 1 *